"*War in the Pews* is indeed a foxhole guide to surviving church conflict. One only has to read the first page to get a feel of the volatility and the variety of church conflicts that can arise. Frank Martin colorfully describes these and moves toward some excellent principles to survival. It will help you in your church."

LYNN ANDERSON
author of *If I Really Believe, Why Do I Have These Doubts?* and *Navigating the Winds of Change*

"Writing with the person in the pew in mind and writing out of his own experience in church struggles, Frank Martin urges church members to work toward peace and unity, thus making their church a more productive, loving place. This book will help us to stay focused and to stop fighting."

LESLIE B. FLYNN
author of *Great Church Fights* and *How to Survive in the Ministry*

"Hooray for Frank Martin! His practical, biblical and commonsensical treatment of this emotionally wrenching subject is like cooling water on a raging inferno. If every congregation in the throes of a battle royal would take time out to read this book, we might see the number of church splits cut dramatically and the cause of Christ advanced considerably."

WILLIAM HENDRICKS
author of *Exit Interviews: Revealing Stories of Why People Are Leaving the Church*

WAR *in the* PEWS

A Foxhole Guide to Surviving Church Conflict

FRANK MARTIN

INTERVARSITY PRESS
DOWNERS GROVE, ILLINOIS 60515

InterVarsity Press® is the book-publishing division of InterVarsity Christian Fellowship®, a student movement active on campus at hundreds of universities, colleges and schools of nursing in the United States of America, and a member movement of the International Fellowship of Evangelical Students. For information about local and regional activities, write Public Relations Dept., InterVarsity Christian Fellowship, 6400 Schroeder Rd., P.O. Box 7895, Madison, WI 53707-7895.

Cover photograph: Michael Goss

ISBN 0-8308-1640-2

Printed in the United States of America ♾

Library of Congress Cataloging-in-Publication Data

Martin, Frank, 1958–
    War in the pews: a foxhole guide to surviving church conflict/
Frank Martin.
       p.   cm.
    Includes bibliographical references.
    ISBN 0-8308-1640-2
    1. Church controversies. 2. Conflict management—Religious aspects—Christianity. 3. Spiritual life—Christianity. I. Title.
BV652.9.M27   1995
250—dc20
                                          94-23855
                                            CIP

21	20	19	18	17	16	5	14	13	12	11	10	9	8	7	6	5	4	3	2	1
12	11	10	09	08	07	06	05	04	03	02	01	00	99	98	97	96	95			

To my parents, Walter & Veronika Martin
two of the most peace-loving people on earth

Acknowledgments

This is not a book I would have thought to write, but it is one that many people need. I hope God will use it to minister to those people.

The idea came over dinner with Andy Le Peau, InterVarsity Press's editorial director. I was seizing the opportunity to pique his interest with some book ideas.

Suddenly he leaned forward and asked, "What are all your friends talking about right now? What's on their minds when you get together with them?"

Almost without thinking, I answered, "Everyone I know is just trying to figure out how to get along in church."

Immediately he latched onto that thought, and together we developed it further. You hold in your hands the end result of that evening's dinner conversation.

Obviously my first words of gratitude go to Andy and his intuitive way of asking questions.

Thanks also to my insightful editor and friend Cynthia Bunch-Hotaling. As always, her instincts were impeccable. She has helped make this a much better book than I could have envisioned or produced alone. And once again my hat's off to the greatest group of book-makers in the world—the keen and kind staff at InterVarsity Press: Ken DeRuiter, Luann Parks,

Nancy Iglesias, Meya Starkey and all the others. What a great group of folks!

A special thanks to those who read through the manuscript and offered comments and advice on making it better, particularly Richard Blackburn, a conflict-resolution specialist, and Ruth Goring, IVP's intuitive copy editor. I only wish I could have done more justice to their suggestions.

Several people went out of their way to help in various ways: Lynn Anderson, Leslie Flynn, Jim Stutzman, Brent Williams, Bill Hendricks and Marlin Thomas, among others. I'm grateful for their kindness.

Thanks to my wonderful in-laws, Bob and Doris Vance, for sharing their stories and insights from years in ministry to others. They've seen their share of conflict in the church—and they've healed many a wounded soldier—yet their faith remains unshaken.

To my fellow strugglers in the faith, my foxhole friends: Rick, Cathryn, Wes, Michele, Jerry, Sharon, Jeff, Jan, Tim, Dierdre, Stuart, Lisa, Dale, Jeannie and many others. Thanks for the stories, prayers and encouragement.

And thanks to my beautiful, patient wife, Ruthie. How could I ever get through a manuscript without her? Her insight and editing make me look much better than I really am. My mistakes are forever our little secret, and for that I'm grateful. Thanks, and I love you.

1

LETTERS FROM A FOXHOLE SURVIVOR

*T*he story is told of a small town nestled deep in the Bible Belt of the American South. The town prided itself in its religious roots, boasting a church on every corner and a Bible on nearly every coffee table. A billboard just inside the city limits welcomed visitors to a town of "old-fashioned values . . . a good place to raise your kids."

But even this town had its bad apples. And when the morning coffee-shop conversation turned to bad apples, usually the person who came to mind was old man Smith, the owner of the gas station just off the highway on the edge of town.

Mr. Smith was the town's outspoken atheist. The only one. And he saw no reason to keep it a secret. So most people had little to do with him. They bought gas at his station, given that it was the only one for miles around, but that was as far as the association went.

On any given Sunday morning the town's streets would be empty and the churches filled. Only Mr. Smith wasn't occupying a pew. He spent Sunday mornings at the gas station, filling tanks for travelers on the highway.

On one such morning a passing tourist stopped to fill up. Getting out for a stretch, he gazed down on the town's many steeples and listened as songs of praise filled the air. He stood silently for a few moments, then turned to old man Smith and remarked, "The people of this town must really love the Lord."

Old man Smith turned to face him with a wry grin. "Well, sir, I wouldn't know about that. All I know is they sure do hate each other."

When Christians Fight

This story may or may not be true (I'm guessing not), but its point is sobering either way. It's sad to think about how many old man Smiths there may be in the world—people who have no faith in God because they see nothing but quarreling among God's people. People who have lost faith in the church because they see so little to envy among the churchgoing "faithful."

Christians argue often, and they seldom fight fairly.

If you are like me, that statement bothers you but doesn't surprise you. Nearly all of us who have grown up in the church, or been in it for more than a few years, have seen firsthand how brutal and mean-spirited fights can be when they occur around and about the church.

I've seen people who are normally easygoing and agreeable begin to lock their jaws and clench their fists over even the smallest issues related to church. A man I knew once threatened to leave the church if the leaders didn't take control of some issues that had upset him. He didn't like to see women passing out bulletins at the front door of the building; he disapproved of congregational singing from inserts in the bulletin instead of hymnbooks. Though he conceded that none of these practices were actually unscriptural, he wondered where such changes would lead. "We have to draw the line somewhere," he insisted.

I saw another man once storm out of a church service, get into his car and drive away. Everyone he left behind was surprised, for he was normally very likable and even-tempered. The sermon that day was from Matthew 19—the story of the rich young ruler who was told to sell his possessions and give to the poor—and this man happened to be a rather wealthy businessman. He was convinced that the lesson was a personal attack from the preacher intended to make him feel guilty. It took several weeks before he was convinced that the minister hadn't singled him out when preparing the sermon.

Chances are good that you've been caught in a few church fights yourself. Most of us have a bucketful of good war stories about churches embroiled in conflict. Let me share just a few more of the stories that have come my way over the last few weeks.

Fellowship-Hall Fiasco

Clayton told me of a very old, conservative church in the Midwest that had spent years raising funds for a fellowship-hall addition to the back of its building. When the time came to break ground, several of the members noticed that the blueprint included a sizable area marked off for a kitchen and dining hall. For some of the members this raised a question: "Is a kitchen in a church building authorized in Scripture?" The debate was low-key at the outset, but within a few weeks camps began to form and polarize.

"A kitchen and dining hall would allow us to have great gatherings and dinners together as a family," came the plea from one camp. "And they would help us entertain unchurched people from the community."

But the other side didn't buy that argument. "If our main purpose on earth is to entertain the community, why don't we just build a casino while we're at it?"

The discussion turned uglier by the day, and soon emotions were at a boiling point. The issue very nearly split the church, until someone mediated and a compromise was found. The fellowship hall was built—and it houses both a large kitchen and a spacious dining hall. But it was built as a separate facility, exactly one foot from the back of the church building.

"When you open the back door of the sanctuary building," Clayton explained, "you see grass on the ground and another door twelve inches in front of you. As you step across the threshold, you can look up and see these two enormous buildings standing exactly one foot away from each other. It looks pretty ridiculous, but at least it solved the problem for both parties involved."

Turning the Tables
Greg told me about an issue that very nearly caused division in his home congregation. "For years the men serving Communion during the service would start at the back of the auditorium and work their way forward," he explained. "Then one day someone decided that they should try having the men line up at the front during the prayer and then work their way toward the back."

The idea seemed reasonable. It wasn't intended to offend; it just seemed logistically more efficient, given the shape of the auditorium. But it wasn't long before complaints started coming. "How are we supposed to concentrate on Communion with a bunch of men staring at us?" complained one person. "All it does is confuse those of us who have been doing it the other way for all these years," said another.

The problem could have been resolved rather simply. Had the church's leaders been aware of the complaints, they could have quickly reverted to the old system and saved a lot of grief. But lines of communication were not very clearly defined. And so they continued to experiment with the program, and the complaints continued to build. Soon a handful of members gathered together and issued an ultimatum: "Stop tinkering with the service or we'll find another church to worship with!"

Some insightful leaders quickly brought the situation under control by returning to the old system, and within a few months the controversy subsided.

"We can look back on it now and laugh at how silly it all seemed," Greg continued, "but at the time it was really intense and frustrating. It looked to most people as if someone was just working at trying to upset the older members by changing things for no reason. And it nearly split the church."

Where Do We Put the Piano?
Cindy tells of a church in the Northeastern United States that had a disagreement over where the piano should be placed in the sanctuary. Some felt that the music sounded better when the pianist played next to the wall to the left of the pulpit. Others were convinced that the right side of the auditorium was the best acoustical choice. So they began experimenting with the piano placement, moving the instrument around from week to week. Both sides were convinced they were right. Soon members of each faction were racing each other to the building on Sunday mornings to see that the piano was "properly" placed before the service started. People began showing up earlier each week, trying to beat the other group to the piano.

One day the disagreement culminated in a physical tug-of-war. Members arrived to find the piano standing in the middle of the sanctuary with a handful of people on either side, shouting, arguing and pulling with all their might toward opposite walls.

I never did hear how the disagreement was settled. I would

have suggested that they buy another piano, so as to have one for each side of the sanctuary, and find another pianist to play along with the first one!

Navel Assault

A church somewhere in the South once commissioned a member to paint a mural on the wall of the teen classroom. The finished picture, based on the creation story, was praised as a beautiful work of art—until someone took a close look and noticed that Adam sported a navel.

"Adam couldn't have had a navel!" this critic exclaimed. "He wasn't born, he was created."

Most fellow parishioners thought the objection was silly and not worth bringing up to the well-intentioned artist. "Besides, maybe God created Adam with a navel," someone suggested. "We have no way of knowing."

The idea of changing the painting was vetoed, and most members assumed the issue had been resolved. But it was only the beginning. "Navelgate" had just begun.

Soon camps formed and polarized over the issue. "Why can't we just change the painting?" was the cry from one side. "You know we're right; you just want to keep it up because you know how much it bothers us."

"What's the big deal?" answered the others. "Altering the mural would be a waste of time and energy."

The conflict escalated into something bigger than anyone had expected, until the church's leaders were finally forced to step in and mediate. When the artist was asked her opinion, the solution came back almost laughably simple: "I'll just paint another leaf on the bush that already covers most of Adam."

A leaf was painted to cover Adam's navel area, and the controversy soon drifted into the nether regions of the congregation's collective memory.

Life in the Foxhole

It's striking how often we can look back on church conflicts and laugh at the pettiness of the issues involved. Granted, not all issues that divide churches can—or should—be considered petty (as I'll discuss in later chapters). But most of the things we argue about are really rather silly and insignificant. After these types of conflicts, almost without exception we wonder later how we could have let ourselves get so caught up in issues that matter so little.

But conflicts, no matter how petty, can tear apart churches, relationships, families and even marriages when they're not dealt with properly. I know firsthand. Over the last few years I've witnessed more than my share of church conflict.

Three years ago a church we were attending went through a split—a very difficult split. The kind where tempers run high and emotions are left frazzled and tense. Lifelong friendships dissolved right in front of us. Even members of the same family took their stand in opposing camps. Though Ruthie and I had both experienced church conflict before, neither of us had been through anything quite so brutal. And we had never before been so personally affected.

I was a deacon and lay leader in the church. Among other things I chaired the church's budget committee, coedited the bimonthly newsletter, wrote and produced most of the brochures and pamphlets the church distributed, taught classes from time to time and oversaw several different ministries. Ruthie was an office volunteer, a contributor to the newsletter and a teacher of children's classes. Together we helped plan the weekly worship services. We were as about as high-profile as laypeople can get. So when the war started heating up, we were caught right on the front lines of battle.

The split didn't happen without warning. We'd been feeling the pangs of conflict for several years before it happened—which probably served to make the open warfare that much more painful. And though some of the conflicts were inevitable, given the mix of ideas and the size of the congregation, most could have been prevented had all of us made the effort to listen and be sensitive to the feelings of others.

No one was really surprised when the split finally occurred. We saw it coming. But that didn't lessen the pain and heartache we felt in the middle of it. One Sunday morning we were one church body, the next week we were two. As simple as that—but about as painless as having your arm severed without anesthesia.

For the most part, the major struggles of that church are now past history. The people are smiling again. They're getting along better than ever. And they've united in their vision to move forward, to reach outward instead of focusing inward.

The wounds are healing. And we've all learned from our mistakes. With God's help, the painful experiences will help the church avoid similar problems in the future. All of us thanked God for the vision and sensitivity of the leaders, as well as their wisdom in guiding the church through the rough storms as best they could.

It could happen again. Nobody is naive about that. In fact, odds are that it probably will—sometime in the future when people forget what the church went through and start to take each other for granted again. Sometime when they let their guards down and allow Satan to wield his tools of divisiveness— pride, self-will, envy, hypocrisy, judgmentalism and the like.

But for now, the church is committed to staying focused on loving each other and being tolerant of one another's shortcomings. They're working at learning unity, not trying to force uniformity.

We're Not Alone
The thing that surprised me most during—and since—our struggles is finding out how commonplace church conflict is. Almost

without exception (I can think of only one) when I shared our story with friends and relatives, I found that they were going through many of the same experiences in their own congregations.

The problem is clearly not limited to certain faiths or denominations. It crosses lines of fellowship and belief—Baptist, Methodist, Catholic, evangelical, charismatic, Church of God, Church of Christ, nondenominational, interdenominational, independent Christian fellowships. No church, it seems, regardless of its faith or doctrine, is immune to conflict.

And though the issues involved are diverse, the symptoms are almost identical. The concerns I heard time and again were all too familiar. "I'm becoming spiritually stagnant," was the cry. "It's affecting my prayer life, my relationship with my wife and kids, and my trust in the church."

We go to church to come closer to God, to build relationships with other Christians, to teach our children the good news of Jesus and pass on the legacy of our faith, and instead we often find ourselves dodging arrows of anger and discontent. We look for a place that will serve as a respite from the world and its problems, and instead we find a whole new world of problems.

If your church is relatively free of conflict and unified in purpose and ideals, feel thankful. And do all you can to see that it stays that way.

But if not—if you're feeling the pains of disunity, if you're lying awake at night wondering when all the strife and struggles will end, if you're tired of dodging hand grenades during the weekly war in the pews at your congregation—then this book is for you. It was conceived and written with your faith and family in mind—from one frontline survivor to another.

Finding God's Direction
God wants his people to get along—to be united in spirit and purpose. Jesus prayed for this harmony, and we should strive to

attain it. But there are times when we need more than a desire to be unified. We need clear guidance and direction.

This book, for the most part, is a set of commonsense suggestions—backed up with biblical examples—meant to help us find that guidance. To help us gain perspective amid the noise and confusion. To help us seek God's will for us through prayer and meditation on his Word. To help us sift through the many voices and find the only one that makes sense—the still, small one. To help us rise above the chaos and find the "peace that passes understanding." To help us delight in the perfect love of God in the midst of an imperfect church.

My family has been forced to do a lot of soul-searching over the last few years. We've experienced every imaginable thought and emotion. We've lost many hours of sleep praying for peace and pleading for guidance. And a lot of good friends have struggled alongside us.

This book is an effort to use the pain we've been through to minister to others. It's not an easy book to write. I've run the risk of opening old and forgotten wounds. That is not my wish, and I've taken every precaution to see that it doesn't happen. Though the stories are all true, I've taken great pains to disguise the identities of the innocent (and the guilty).

Right now there is a mound of dirt where our family's foxhole used to be. We've moved on to use our gifts in another church home, but the role we played in helping our earlier church through its struggles has prepared us well for the future.

For us, and our former church, the battle is over. But if your war is still waging—if you've found yourself caught in a deep trench without a white flag in sight—then take heart. There is a way to find safety in the chaos.

You may not be able to frame terms of peace that will persuade everyone to stop waging the war, but you can certainly prevent yourself from becoming a casualty of it.

PART I

WHEN THE
BATTLE
LINES
HAVE BEEN
DRAWN

2

ANATOMY OF A CHURCH FIGHT

*T*he story made headlines for the better part of a month in a small town just outside New York City. The day the story broke, the front page carried a picture of a church building torn in half. Written across the top of the picture in large letters was the word *DIVIDED*. The headline read, "Church Locked, Chained. Trustees Shut Church. Deacons Will Try to Reopen It."

A few days later, another headline appeared: "Ousted Pastor Holds Sidewalk Service."

Days later: "Deacon Cuts Chains Locking Church Door."

Again: "Church Re-chained from Inside."

A few weeks passed before another headline appeared: "Members Battle over Control of Church. Judge Puts Minister's Fate in Congregation's Hands."[1]

I never did learn the final outcome, but regardless of who won, everyone lost. Especially the cause of Christ.

Another newspaper in Wales carried the ongoing story of a feuding church in search of a new pastor. One headline stretched across the top of the page: "Hallelujah! Two Jacks in One Pulpit." An excerpt from the story read:

Yesterday the two opposition groups both sent ministers to the pulpit. Both spoke simultaneously, each trying to shout above the other. Both called for hymns, and the congregation sang two—each side trying to drown out the other. Then the groups began shouting at each other. Bibles were raised in anger. The Sunday morning service turned into bedlam. Through it all, the two preachers continued trying to outshout each other with their sermons.

Eventually a deacon called a policeman. Two came in and began shouting for the congregation to be quiet. They advised the forty persons in the church to return home. The rivals filed out, still arguing.

Last night one of the groups called a "let's-be-friends" meeting. It broke up in argument.[2]

These episodes remind me of the church pastor who came home one day to find his daughter arguing with her friends in the bedroom. From the front hallway he could hear them yelling and calling each other names, so he quickly made his way up the stairs.

"What's going on in here?" he asked as he entered the room.

His five-year-old looked up at him and smiled. "It's okay, Daddy. We're just playing church!"

No doubt about it. Conflict in the church is a very real problem. Too often over the years Christians have gained a reputation of being a group that preaches love and kindness but practices discord and dissension. It's not that we don't love Christ, it's just that we can't seem to get along with each other.

Author Gerald Sittser has some disturbing news about conflict in the church:

Many denominations in America are strained to the breaking point because their members disagree so sharply over . . . issues. Catholics are quarreling over papal authority, birth control, women in church office and academic freedom. Protestants are divided between liberal and conservative in almost every major denomination. In *The Struggle for America's Soul* Robert Wuthnow argues that the split between conservative and liberal is the dominant conflict in the Protestant church today. However destructive these disagreements are, there is little indication that resolution is anywhere in sight. If anything, the conflict is just heating up, with both sides poised to fight over any number of issues. And neither, it seems, is ready to compromise.[3]

According to a survey conducted by Jerrien Gunnink, "more than 30,000 Protestant churches in the United States alone are in a serious conflict at any given time." He goes on:

A new genre of specialists has emerged, with the purpose of leading a church through dissension and resolving the internal conflict. Troubled churches are led through "assertiveness training," "negotiating sessions," "communication techniques," "listening skills," "confrontational methods," "peacemaking," and a host of other formulas designed to bring harmony and peace.[4]

We're having so much trouble getting along in church that we've created a need for a new specialization for pastors. Most seminaries and Bible colleges now prepare future preachers for conflict through studies on conflict resolution and mediation.

Why Do We Do It?

But why do we do it? Why do we fight so often and so bitterly in the house of God? Why does it seem as though people who can put up with almost any change or debate in the workplace or at the social club will refuse to even listen to a differing point of view from a fellow Christian?

The one place on earth that we hope will be a sanctuary from conflict often becomes a breeding ground for it.

Though there are probably many factors involved in the dynamics of that problem, the best explanation I've found comes from Hugh Halverstadt, professor of ministry at McCormick Theological Seminary:

Indeed, why do church folk who may fight fair at work often fight dirty at church? Apparently, certain forces shape the feelings and behaviors of parties in church conflicts.

For one thing, parties' core identities are at risk in church conflicts. Spiritual commitments and faith understandings are highly inflammatory because they are central to one's psychological identity. When Christians differ over beliefs or commitments, they may question or even condemn one another's spirituality or character. Their self-esteem is on the line. That is why parties slip so easily into taking differences personally, even launching personal attacks. When church folk feel that their worldview or personal integrity is being questioned or condemned, they often become emotionally violent and violating. Any means are used to justify their goal of emotional self-protection.[5]

In other words, we fight so readily in church because church is more than just something we do or someplace we go. Our faith is our identity, and church is the embodiment of our faith. It is not what we do, it is who we are. And when someone questions what we do in church, they are questioning more than our actions or traditions. They are questioning the very essence of our faith. They are questioning *us*. In effect, they are questioning our spirituality—perhaps even our salvation. Thus we can be extremely sensitive and irrational when it comes to conflict in the church.

Like many, I had to learn this lesson the hard way. Years ago I volunteered to serve on a worship planning committee of a church. One of the first things our group decided was to try some innovative things during the Sunday-morning services. We weren't looking to shake up any of the longtime members, we just thought some variety would be nice. So we began using some contemporary songs interspersed with Scripture reading. We also planned some drama and special music. In many churches this would have gone over quite well, but this was a very conservative, traditional fellowship. The changes were not met with open arms.

Complaints came in from every angle. We had no idea how—or why—we had offended so many in such a short time. Our initial reaction was to defend the changes as "necessary." "We're only trying to breathe new life into a stale service," we said.

Wrong answer.

"There's nothing wrong with the way we've been doing it all these years," came the response, time and again.

I remember being very critical of the complainers. I felt they were being selfish and inflexible for no apparent reason. *They're just stubborn and uncaring—intent on getting their way,* I thought. And many of them were. But as I look back, I can see that I was as much in the wrong as they were. I was being as stubborn and uncaring as any one of them.

In many cases they were less concerned about the changes than about what they perceived as our elitist attitudes. By calling their services stale and in need of new life, we were not questioning their methods but their spiritual depth. In effect we were calling *them* stale and boring. And in doing so, we set off their defense mechanisms.

Many church conflicts can be traced back to those same dynamics. When two people disagree over a tradition, an interpretation of Scripture or a doctrinal position, they are not just arguing a point, they are taking each other to task intellectually, theologically and spiritually—at least in their minds.

When we question someone's traditions and beliefs, we are stomping on some very sacred ground. And we're setting ourselves up for trouble.

Personality Clashes

Of course there are many other dynamics at work when Christians argue, and I couldn't begin to list here all of the things that cause friction. Chapter thirteen will discuss some of the more common "peace-busters" in churches. Suffice it to say here that most conflicts in the church can be traced to one basic point: people are different. We are a diverse society with differing ideas, personalities, agendas and beliefs. No two people on earth will agree on every issue, whether it comes under politics, life philosophy or religion. And because of that fact, conflict—in life and in church—is inevitable.

Take my marriage. My wife, Ruthie, and I love each other dearly, but we are very different people. She is a thinker, an analyzer and a list-maker. I'm an off-the-scale feeler and generally fly by the seat of my pants. I've never made a list in my life, and I usually lose the ones Ruthie gives me (accidentally, of course). She's a saver, very frugal with money. I'm a spender, terrible with budgets.

These differences in our personalities have caused their share of conflicts in our home. We're on opposite sides of many issues, and it would be very easy for us to allow these differences to tear us apart and ruin our marriage. We saw early in the relationship how easy it would be for that to happen. But we were—and are—determined to make our marriage work, to grow closer to each other each day instead of farther apart. We love each other enough to keep a close watch on our tongues, thoughts and attitudes.

We still disagree, but we keep the disputes in perspective and under tight control. Sometimes that means working through a conflict until we've come to an agreement; other times it means simply agreeing to disagree. The day may come when a conflict grows out of our control, forcing us to consider bringing in a third party to help us work through it. Thankfully, we haven't had to do that, but if the need arose, we would both be willing. Our marriage is much too important for us to let our pride stand in the way of our love for and devotion to each other.

The same dynamics are at work in a church family. There will be many people at church who clash with us on a personal and intellectual level. We will disagree often and on many different issues. The question is, will we let those disagreements tear us apart, or will we work at finding solutions? Do we care enough for each other to work at finding a good compromise? Are we willing to agree to disagree if the need arises? Is our love great enough to motivate us to do whatever possible to keep peace and unity within the family? And if we need to leave, can we do so in a spirit of love and humility instead of bitterness?

Conflict in the church is inevitable. Dissension and division are not!

Danger or Opportunity

As Ruthie and I have seen in our marriage, and as most conflict managers will assert, conflict is not necessarily a bad thing. It can be and has been used as a tool for growth and deeper understanding. As Speed Leas and Paul Kittlaus point out, any church free of problems "would be a dumb, shallow and depressing kind of place."[6] Conflict, they say, should not be looked on with fear, anxiety or guilt, but should be seen as an exciting challenge.

In fact, the Chinese written word for "crisis" is made up of two different characters—*wei*, which means "danger," and *chi*, which means "opportunity." "The blueprint of an open universe," they call it.[7] A world free of conflict would be a world void of growth and insight.

Richard Wolf puts it another way: "Not every conflict is necessarily neurotic. Some is normal and healthy. The tension between what is and what ought to be—the gap between reality and ideal—is indispensable to well-being. Every challenge carries tension within itself. We do not need a tensionless state, but a challenging goal and purpose."[8]

The goal in dealing with conflict in the church, then, should not be to eliminate it completely. The goal is to manage those conflicts openly and with sensitivity. And since one of the main purposes of a church is to help people grow spiritually and emotionally, conflict can be seen as just one more avenue to help in facilitating that growth.

That can be a comforting thought. Especially if you've found yourself in the middle of one of those thirty thousand churches embroiled in conflict. The knowledge that conflict can lead to growth doesn't let us off the hook when we argue—especially over petty issues—but it does help to understand the dynamics at work when Christians argue.

Keeping the Peace

In a sense I suppose it should be encouraging that Christians take their faith so seriously. What would it say about us if we took a "couldn't care less" attitude about things that happen within Christ's body? At least we care. Indifference would be the greater sin.

But that doesn't solve our problem. Knowing why we fight is one thing; managing those fights is another. How do we effectively keep conflict in the church under control? What can we do to curtail divisive problems before they arise? How do we go about settling conflicts quickly and conclusively when they do arise? And how do we keep church fights from diverting us from our mission and purpose as people of God?

Those and other questions are addressed in the next chapter. Entire books have been written on the subject, so I won't presume to cover it exhaustively here. But I will give some practical guidelines—guidelines that can be found within the pages of Scripture.

3

THE ONE-
MINUTE
CONFLICT
MANAGER

*T*he book of 1 Samuel contains a beautiful story that illustrates how the simple, sincere efforts of one person can literally turn armies away from a conflict. It has much to teach all of us about how to effectively manage conflict. The story is that of Nabal and Abigail.

Nabal is described as a "surly and mean" man, while his wife, Abigail, is said to have been "intelligent and beautiful." Nabal was a very wealthy sheep shearer residing in the Desert of Maon. While his servants herded his flock of one thousand goats and three thousand sheep, King David's men protected them. Day and night they served as a wall around the shepherds so that none of Nabal's livestock would be taken.

Then one day David sent a group of ten messengers to Nabal, asking for a small favor of food and goods for his army. Given that David's men had taken such good care of Nabal's men and livestock, he didn't think the request unreasonable. But Nabal refused and sent the men away, hurling insults at them.

David was livid and immediately mounted an army of four hundred men to wipe out Nabal and every male member of his house and staff. "He has paid me back evil for good," David said. Then he and the army took off toward Nabal's land to take revenge.

When Abigail heard of the confrontation, she wasted no time in coming to the rescue. She took a generous supply of provisions, loaded the goods onto donkeys and went to meet David. When she reached the approaching army, she dismounted from her donkey and bowed on her knees before David. At his feet, she said, "My lord, let the blame be on me alone. . . . May my lord pay no attention to that wicked man Nabal. He is just like his name—his name is Fool, and folly goes with him."

As she knelt before David, his heart began to soften. He accepted her gifts, praising her for her "good judgment," and called off the assault.

During the entire episode, Nabal, the true culprit, was busy throwing a party and getting drunk, oblivious to problems he had caused—as well as the fate that had nearly overcome him (see 1 Samuel 25).

Principles for Conflict Resolution
Though most of us won't have to face an army for our harsh words and poor judgment, it still is always good to have people like Abigail around when we need them. Every church could use a few people like that. Especially since there are so many Nabals among us.

And what were the tools Abigail used to turn away David's wrath? They are tools we all have at our disposal—though some may be hard to wield.

☐ *Humility.* She humbled herself before him and apologized, even though she was not the one in the wrong. Abigail was willing to bow down before David and ask forgiveness on behalf of her husband. How many of us would be willing to do the same? Most of us have a hard time practicing humility even when we know we've been in the wrong. But to do so when we are innocent, or on behalf of a friend or husband? That's true humility!

☐ *Gentleness.* Proverbs 15:1 says, "A gentle answer turns away wrath." Abigail was calm and kind in the face of adversity. While kneeling before King David, she offered him the gifts she had brought, gently asking him to spare her husband. And within a few short minutes her kind words and attitude had melted David's wrath like butter.

☐ *Sincerity.* She was truly sympathetic to the wrong David had suffered at the tongue of her husband. And her sincerity showed clearly.

☐ *Restitution.* She wanted to make things right with the king—to do more than simply apologize, to make good on what was owed him for his past help.

☐ *Swiftness.* She didn't dawdle. When she learned of the storm brewing, she quickly went into action. She didn't wait until things were out of control.

By keeping her head and her commitments clear, Abigail was able to save many lives and avert what was sure to be a devastating confrontation.

All of us can follow her lead. We may not be experts in conflict resolution, but we can certainly use our cool heads and common sense to dispel conflicts when they arise. And the more people in the church who are willing to do that, the calmer things will be.

Me, a Conflict Manager?
God can use each of us as an agent of peace, both in the church and in the world. In fact, Scripture demands that in all we do,

regardless of our agenda, we work toward peace and love and unity.

Wonderful books have been written for church leaders on how to mediate and arbitrate disputes in the church—most of them about four hundred pages of fine print analyzing the principles of conflict resolution. The ones I've read are packed with good advice for ministers and church leaders. You'll find them in the list of suggested readings in appendix A at the back.

But this book is aimed at those of us in the pews—the grunt soldiers buried in foxholes on the frontlines of battle. Few of us can take a high-profile role in dealing with church conflicts. But most of us are affected by the struggles, either directly or indirectly. We want to help, but we don't want to risk getting in the way and making things worse.

What can we do on a practical level to help make our church a more peaceful, productive place? How can we be a unifying element in the middle of a fragmented church family?

Here are a few simple principles that can help you and me become agents of peace when war wages in the pews.

Don't Take Yourself (and Others) Too Seriously

Jesus doesn't expect us to always be right, but he does expect us to always be loving. He didn't pray that his people would be doctrinally perfect but that they would be unified in spirit.

"The majority of church disputes," writes Karen Jordan, "center on personal preferences, not moral issues."[1] Too often we act as if every disagreement we have with a fellow believer were an issue of scriptural purity, when actually we're only debating opinions.

In my experience, the people who are constantly in conflict are inevitably those who take themselves much too seriously. I call them "jot-and-tittle people." Every minor issue must be resolved to their liking or they aren't happy. They can't stand unresolved arguments and will never agree to disagree—they'd rather continue arguing until someone wins.

One jot-and-tittle person I know spends his time at church going from person to person looking for a good argument. When he has a disagreement with a leader or a certain church policy, he wants to know how everyone else feels about the issue. And if they don't agree with him on every point, he stands arguing until they do—or at least until they concede. Needless to say, he's built quite a reputation. People go out of their way to avoid him.

Another person I know from a church in Texas is the exact opposite. Sandy is always carefree and fun to be around. He spends much of his time laughing at himself. He never takes himself—or anyone else—too seriously. Everyone smiles to see him. Sandy is Teflon for conflict—it rolls right off him. He refuses to give conflict the foothold it needs to cause him strife.

We could all learn from Sandy. When it comes to keeping conflict in check, one key is to learn to laugh at ourselves—to not take ourselves and our opinions too seriously.

Look for the Good in Others

Paul wrote in his letter to the Philippians, "Whatever is true, whatever is noble, whatever is right, whatever is pure, whatever is lovely, whatever is admirable—if anything is excellent or praiseworthy—think about such things" (4:8).

But when churches get into a conflict mode, people start watching for trouble. They expect something to happen, and so it usually does. *I wonder what so-and-so's going to say this morning,* they think. And others are thinking the same thing. So before long, even if so-and-so says nothing, a disagreement arises.

Negative attitudes have split many a church family down the middle. One of the best ways to combat negativism is through optimistic thinking—taking Paul's advice and looking for the good in others instead of the bad.

Open Lines of Communication (and Be Humble!)

My good friend Ron told me of a situation that arose in a church he once attended. He had been teaching a class on Christian living and noticed that one man in the group seemed hostile toward him. No matter what passage or point Ron brought up, this man would take him to task—usually disrupting the lesson in the process. Ron was baffled by the man's behavior, so he decided to talk to him about it. "I sense that you have a problem with me," he told the man, "and I thought we might be able to discuss it."

Without hesitation, the man tore into him. "Look," he said, "I don't like your class, I don't like the way you teach, and basically I just don't like you!"

He gave no reason or explanation. He just didn't like Ron.

Ron was very hurt by this confrontation. Here was a brother who was antagonistic toward him for no apparent reason. He had no idea what to do about this hostile brother, so he simply began to pray daily. He prayed for guidance in handling the situation. Soon, he says, he felt God calling him to pray with this man as well as for him. It wasn't a pleasing prospect, since the man had been hateful, rude and insensitive. But still, Ron knew he needed to follow the Spirit's leading. So he humbled himself and asked the man to meet him for prayer.

Obviously it was an awkward situation for both of them, but the man agreed. And so they bowed in prayer. They met the next week and prayed again. Every week for several months, these two men met and prayed together, until they became good friends.

And it all started with a simple, brave act of humility.

In the middle of a conflict with a brother or sister in Christ, usually our state of mind is far from meekness and humility. We're usually looking for a way to get the upper hand—to come up with the perfect comeback to their accusations. But a true warrior of peace, an Abigail, knows that loving confrontation, coupled with honest humility, is a powerful tool for managing conflict.

Apply Your Talents Toward Unity
One church I know of was feeling the pains of disunity due to a very high turnover rate in the congregation. Over the previous few years many people had moved out of the area and others had moved in to take their place. It was a very unstable environment for building relationships, and many of the members lamented that they had few friends in the church.

One woman noticed the problem and wanted to do something about it. So she approached the leaders with the idea of having a weekly time of fellowship before morning service. She envisioned a fifteen-minute break between classes and the worship service when members could enjoy donuts, coffee and conversation, and she volunteered to use her organizational talents in helping put it together. The leaders agreed, and today the coffee break has become one of the church's most effective and enjoyable times of fellowship. It has clearly helped to unify the congregation.

Five years ago several people in our church were concerned about the need for better communication between leaders and members. Many members were feeling alienated from the church and its many programs and ministries.

One day Michele, a good friend and writer, came to me with the idea of starting a church newsletter. It would help open up lines of communication, she explained, and it would give the elders and ministry leaders a forum for keeping the congregation abreast of their activities.

She and I began organizing the newsletter, and before long we had created an effective means of communication for the congregation. The newsletter became a powerful tool to unify the church through keeping people informed.

If you are aware of specific problems that are causing conflict in your own church, maybe you could be the one to patch that hole in the dike. Maybe you can use your talents and influence to help unify your church—start a fellowship ministry, organize small groups, help teach in the nursery, begin home evangelism studies, or do whatever else needs doing.

Paul wrote to the Colossians, "Whatever you do, work at it with all your heart, as working for the Lord, not for men, since you know that you will receive an inheritance from the Lord as a reward." (Colossians 3:23-24). What we do in church we do because of our love for the Lord and our desire to see his body unified. No matter how simple or hidden our work is, the Lord notices. And though others may not mention it, they benefit as well.

Do you complain about problems—or do you apply your creativity to helping solve them? If you have committed yourself to being part of the solution, your church is blessed.

Stay Centered on Jesus
In *The Body* Chuck Colson writes:

Disunity would be understandable if Christianity were nothing more than a set of creeds and confessions. But Christianity is more than these. It is centered in the One who professes to be ultimate reality, the personal God who gives us life and meaning and who calls us to be His body at work in the world. If we really understand this, disunity becomes impossible.[2]

Ultimately division and disunity come when we take our eyes off Jesus and center them instead on ourselves, on our own desires and agendas. When we lose sight of God's purpose for the church, when we forget our mission, when we begin to focus inward, we begin to quarrel and argue and divide loyalties.

The greatest thing you and I can do for the cause of peace is to focus on Jesus. Everything else takes its proper place when brought into the light of his presence.

When We've Done All We Can

There are obviously many other aspects of being agents of peace in the middle of conflict. Topping that list is the need to make sure you are not part of the problem—that you're not adding in any way to the strife your church is suffering (more on that in chapter fourteen). The last thing your church—or any other church—needs is more Nabals hanging around, causing dissension at every turn.

Conflict in churches is not always caused by poor leadership, bad theology or stubborn members. Sometimes it's simply that a church family has gotten into a bad habit of bickering and doesn't know how to stop it. Members begin to argue over little things, then they argue over bigger issues. Complaining becomes familiar and habitual, and before you know it the church is in a downward spiral, bickering more by the day over even the slightest offenses.

We've all felt the same dynamics in our families. Even the most close-knit family feels the strain of cabin fever from time to time. Familiarity breeds conflict. And conflict can easily breed disunity.

Being aware of that dynamic is the first step in guarding against it—whether in a family or in a church. A healthy amount of conflict is good for us, as long as it doesn't turn into selfish bickering and division.

But some church families become so bogged down in strife and dissension that it seems beyond us to gain back the perspective we need. Bickering becomes so commonplace that people expect it. More than that, they start to enjoy it. Some people thrive on conflict, and a church embedded in strife only feeds those desires. Before long the downward spiral seems unstoppable.

Insightful leaders know that during these times, bringing in a specialist in conflict resolution is probably in order—in some cases a necessity. Like marriage partners trying to overcome years of hurt and resentment, we sometimes are physically and emotionally unable to cope on our own. We need an outside professional to help us repair the relationship.

There are people and organizations devoted to that very purpose. Appendix B at the back of this book is a list of some of the avenues you might take to locate a professional church healer—someone with the tools and the wherewithal to identify your needs and facilitate the healing process. These "conflict doctors" can bring fresh insight to your church about what may lie at the root of your conflicts. And they are willing to stay around until they've found the right medicine to heal. Afterward they'll equip the church's leaders to head off similar problems in the future.

If your church seems to be in a downward spiral of conflict, talk to your leaders about looking into bringing in a third party. Let's not ever let our pride keep us from getting help when we need it—whether in our homes or in our churches.

It *is* possible to repair a strife-torn church. And it is possible to move forward with a new sense of unity and purpose. But only if everyone involved is willing to do their share.

God doesn't expect us to be perfect, but he does expect us to be loving and peaceable. He invites us to practice the life of heaven right here on earth.

4

HOLDING YOURSELF TOGETHER WHEN YOUR CHURCH IS FALLING APART

*F*ew people ever become as involved in their local church as Jim and Peggy were. For twenty years they worked and worshiped faithfully at the small congregation they called home. Peggy taught Sunday school, sang in the choir and served as a church trustee. Jim was a deacon, a youth-group leader and chair of the budget committee. He also served on numerous other committees. They were as high-profile as laypeople get.

Then one day the church hired a new pastor. At first everyone was thrilled with the decision, including Jim and Peggy. But before long they began seeing things they didn't like. Though the pastor was a good speaker, he was very controlling. The power previously held by lay leaders began dwindling away. The church committees were beginning to feel the strain of ineffectiveness.

Peggy noticed a sneakiness in the pastor's conducting of church business. He had a way of getting what he wanted when he wanted it, and often his methods were dishonest and under-handed. Basically Jim and Peggy lost respect for him but felt powerless to do anything about their disappointment.

For five years Jim and Peggy maintained their commitment to the church, in spite of the shrinking congregation and the growing feeling of unrest within the membership. It was difficult for them to work in a church that they felt so discouraged about, but they remained for the sake of their kids and the friendships they had built. Still, they were unhappy. And with each passing month their unhappiness grew.

Finally their thirteen-year-old daughter expressed her feelings of alienation from the youth group. By now the teen population had dwindled, and many of her close friends had left. Those who remained were either unruly or unkind to the other kids. She told her parents she was ready to leave, and that was all the prompting they needed. The next Sunday they withdrew their membership and began visiting other congregations.[1]

A Struggle for Power

Tom and Carla had spent sixteen years worshiping with a me-dium-sized, conservative congregation in the Midwest. They were active members with many good friendships, and their teenage children grew to be leaders in the youth group. Tom ran a successful business and was a strong financial supporter of the church. More than a few times he had come through in times of low funds and needed repairs.

For most of their time there they were happy. The congrega-tion was united in purpose and ideals. Carla and Tom were growing spiritually, and their kids were on track as well.

But somewhere along the way the church started feeling the

pains of disunity. Conflicts that had once been handled rather quickly and easily began to drag out and build up from week to week. More and more people vocalized their discontent. Factions began to form over even the smallest matters of disagreement.

Carla and Tom also noticed power struggles among the church leaders. After the church appointed new elders, rumors of infighting began to circulate. Before long it was apparent that the rumors were true. More than a few times during a Sunday-morning service a disgruntled elder went to the pulpit to disavow ownership in a policy or decision. One particularly hostile elder even interrupted a large Sunday-school class to discredit the teacher.

Tom and Carla wanted to stay committed to the church, riding out the storm until the winds of division subsided. And for several years they did stay. They continued to serve and worship, trying as best they could to steer clear of the conflict. But after a while it became too much for them. They were emotionally drained, and their children were beginning to feel out of place as the conflict crept into the youth program.

One day they decided they'd had enough. So they left and began attending another church. When last I heard from them they still had not placed membership. They wanted to make sure they would not soon have a repeat of their previous situation, so they decided to take their time before making a decision.

Divided Loyalties

Ian loved the singles group at the large church he had been attending. Its activities kept him busy several nights of the week—and that was exactly what he wanted. He had few interests outside of work, church and finding the right mate. The group's busy schedule allowed him much time and opportunity to pursue the last item on that list.

As the years passed the group grew stronger. But turmoil started brewing in the church over some theological and doctrinal issues. The conflict was quiet at first, but eventually it started seeping into the Sunday-morning services. For the most part the singles kept to themselves, and the conflict seldom bothered them. It was a carefree and idealistic group, mostly oblivious to the extent of the rising conflict.

But the conflict was serious, and soon the church split down the middle. Within days after a large group left and formed another church several miles away, the phone calls began. The splinter group was intent on drawing as many people as possible away from the original church. An old friend called Ian, encouraging him to leave and worship with the new congregation. The other singles in the group received calls as well.

Now, in spite of all its efforts to remain detached, the singles group was caught in the middle of the conflict. Each member was forced to make a decision about where his or her loyalties would be placed. Opinions were divided.

Ian decided to stay. Others, including the leader of the singles ministry, decided to leave. Friendships were strained; some were destroyed.

For a time the group at the old church tried to reorganize, but things were never the same. The church's leaders had more pressing needs to worry about, and no one came forward to head up the singles ministry. So the group began to dwindle and die. Soon only a handful of singles remained, and the busy calendar of activities was a thing of the past.

Ian was troubled. He wanted to remain loyal to the church, to help it reunite and rebuild. But he also wanted to be part of a group of single friends—quite honestly, a group where he'd have a chance to meet someone he'd like to marry. Here he was in his mid-twenties with a successful career, but in his church he had little opportunity to meet young women or make friends. Yet he felt loyal to his church and felt it truly needed him.

He didn't feel right about defecting to the splinter group, given its poor attitudes and divisive motives during its departure. But he did know of another church in the area with a dynamic singles ministry. Some of his friends were attending there, and the draw was very hard to resist.

For close to a year Ian remained in his church out of loyalty. He hoped things would get better, but they never did. Morale was low, and the only friends he had were married and busy with work and family. Physically Ian was still a member. But emotionally he had left months earlier.

Slowly he began withdrawing from church involvement. And one day he made up his mind to move on. The singles group at his new church welcomed him warmly, and soon Ian wondered aloud why it had taken him so long to leave.

The Million-Dollar Question

These stories and their outcomes could be endlessly debated. Were these people justified in leaving their church homes? Did they do the right thing? Were their motives wrong? Were their expectations too high? Did they sell out and retreat when they should have dug in their heels and persevered? Was personal happiness more important to them than doctrinal purity? Are they just examples of the consumer mentality that has become so common in Western society?

Churches are supposed to be like families to us. We're supposed to learn how to work through our disagreements and move forward in love and unity. We're supposed to do all we can to keep the peace. And we certainly want to do all we can to help our church be a sign of God's kingdom in the world.

But there is a point at which we've done all we can do. There is a time to decide that God could use us better elsewhere—at another church home. Sometimes the best thing we can do for our church is to move on. And sometimes God calls us to do just that.

If you feel that you've honestly done all you can to make your church the best it can be, but still you struggle with feelings of discontent, maybe it is time to move on. If you've worked at keeping the peace, at helping your church get past the conflicts and move forward, but still the war wages all around, maybe it is time to consider retiring from the battle. Maybe God wants you to use your talents and energy elsewhere.

It's possible to wear out one's welcome in a church. And there are times when God simply has plans in mind for us elsewhere. When that time comes, we need to be willing to follow wherever he might lead—no matter how painful it might seem.

The million-dollar question is, How do we know when—and if—that time has come?

The answer is, When you see God clearly leading you in that direction.

All You Can Do Is All You Can Do

I identify with the people whose stories I've told—I've been right where they were. The questions they were forced to face became all too familiar to my family. The conflict in our church stretched our loyalties to the breaking point. It was the toughest dilemma we've ever faced.

As a deacon and leader, I loved the church. I wanted to do all I could to strengthen it—to help it become the kind of vibrant, relevant church that Christ would want it to be. But as a Christian, a husband and a father, I had another, greater responsibility—to my faith and my family.

How could I prevent the problems at church from bleeding over into our home life? How could I keep the strained relationships at church from straining my relationship with Christ? Would disagreements in church find their way into my home, my family, my marriage?

Was God trying to lead us elsewhere?

As I pondered the problems, I realized that I could deal with any amount of conflict that might come up in the church. But I was not willing to let the conflict break the bond of faith within my family circle. The problems must not influence my children to become disillusioned and lose faith.

It can happen more easily than we might think. I've seen it happen, and chances are you have too. It's a heartbreaking thing to witness.

The next section of this book is intended to address these dilemmas. Later chapters will discuss some dynamics of true Christian unity. But for now we're going to focus on us. On our families, our faith. On those of us sitting in the pews week after week trying desperately to keep our faith and family together while the hand grenades fly.

It may be God's will for you to quietly slip out the back door of your church and find another congregation to call home. Or he may want you to stay and become an agent of peace and understanding—a dynamic leader in a church lacking direction and leadership. He may call you to be a quiet and calm model of reason in a cacophony of unreasonable voices.

The important thing to remember is, God does have a purpose for you—for each of us. It's our job to seek out that purpose. To listen for him amid the noise and confusion, and to be willing to follow wherever he may lead.

The next few chapters offer a six-step plan for survival. It's a plan that's designed to help us seek out God's guidance in the middle of a struggling church—to help us answer the million-dollar question that plagues so many families in strife-torn churches.

The plan draws on many sources—the wisdom of friends, experts and Scripture. And of personal experience. I've *lived* this book. These principles have worked well to keep my family on track and our church problems in perspective.

I pray that God will use these principles in your life as he has in ours. And that through the strife and conflict your faith will not only survive, but thrive.

PART II

A SIX-STEP
PLAN FOR
SURVIVAL

5

STEP ONE:
RETREAT
AND
REGROUP

*I*n our church, though the issues that were causing dissension were varied, most of them came down to one basic question: Should we change the style and format of our worship services to meet the needs of a changing culture, or should we remain the same?

Some of us wanted to see a more contemporary flair to the way we did church. We were excited about many new songs and wanted to integrate them into our services. Though we loved the old hymns, we saw how little meaning they have to today's young, unchurched families. We wanted to reevaluate the church's traditional, low-key order of worship. Why not try some drama, interpretive readings or special music?

But others had no desire to change. They loved the old songs and traditions. They wondered aloud if we were not trying to change just for the sake of change, and if somehow the message of the gospel wasn't going to get diluted in the process of reevaluation. Though they acknowledged the fast-paced changes in society, they felt that the church should remain the same—a stabilizing force in an unstable culture.

Both arguments had their virtues. Neither group had the right to point a condescending finger at the other (though that did happen). And neither could say that its preference was somehow more spiritual than the other preferences (though, again, it happened).

Still, the problem is and was very real—for our church and for countless others across the country. And since we met each week to worship and celebrate together, the problem surfaced often. Resentment had a way of building from week to week.

The dissension carried a great deal of emotional weight in our family because of our heavy involvement in church work. Ruthie and I had been committed to a number of different projects and ministries over the years—heading up ministries, publishing the church newsletter, helping plan the services. Much of our time was dedicated to working for and with the church.

As much as we loved what we were doing, we saw that we were paying a price. Problems in the church often spilled over into our home life. Because we were so close to the situation, it was often difficult not to take the conflicts personally.

Many times we would come home exhausted after the morning services. "I'm so tired of the constant tension," Ruthie would tell me. "Why does it always have to feel so awkward at church?"

We wondered often if we were in the right church. Was God trying to tell us to move on? Did he want us to stay and be content with the way things were? Or did he want us to continue to work toward change? We honestly didn't know.

More than anything, we needed God's guidance. So we set out to look for his will in the midst of the confusion.

A Time to Retreat and Regroup

What we did first was not a conscious, reasoned choice. It was more a knee-jerk reaction: we took a few days to retreat and regroup.

Weighed down with the stress of conflict, we decided to back away from our involvement and try to sort out the situation. Between work, the children, committee meetings, projects and various church activities, we had been so hurried and frazzled that before we could even think clearly about the issues, we needed to slow down our motors and retreat.

So we "closed the zoo." We retreated into our home for a few days to just relax and talk and think. And pray.

When Sunday rolled around, we even decided to visit another church. Though I don't necessarily recommend that you do the same, it was important for us, because of our high visibility in the congregation, to steer clear of any conflict during our time of rest.

We didn't need to hear outside voices during this time. We wanted to clear our hearts and minds of any hint of discontent.

This was time we needed to ourselves—one or two weeks to reflect on our own needs and feelings. It was a time to take inventory of our spiritual and emotional health, to see how we were faring—and especially how our children were holding up—in the middle of all the fighting.

How were our children being affected by the church conflicts that arose in their presence? Were they able to separate the love of God and the joy of knowing him from the struggles they were witnessing among God's people?

We needed to consider our own spiritual health. How were the struggles at church affecting our prayer life, our love for the church, our love for other Christians, our personal relationship with God?

Slowing Down to Look for Guidance

We didn't see the wisdom in the decision at the time, but we've since come to see that it was an important step in our quest for guidance.

Bill Hybels, in his book *Too Busy Not to Pray,* talks of the importance of slowing down when life gets confusing:

I see pastors, elders, church board members operating at the same relentless pace as everyone else. Never a dull moment; never a reflective moment either. Frightened, I ask myself, "Where does the still, small voice of God fit into our hectic lives? When do we allow him to lead and guide and correct and affirm? And if this seldom or never happens, how can we lead truly authentic Christian lives?"[1]

Someone once said, "If you want to get something done, give it to the busiest person you can find." That statement rings doubly true when it comes to church work. Once you become known as an eager volunteer, a "get-it-done" kind of person, most churches will wear you out with the many tasks that need doing. There are pamphlets to be distributed, sick people to visit, bulletins to be printed, classrooms to be decorated, lawns to be mowed, floors to be scrubbed, special events to prepare for . . . the list goes on and on.

And that's not a bad thing, mind you. Any lively, faithful church is reaching outward enough to create work for anyone and everyone interested. A church building that is empty and dead during the week is likely doing little to serve the community or to lead people into deeper knowledge of God.

The problem comes when you find yourself buried in involvement. When you've volunteered your life to the limit.

I happen to believe that churches should set up policies to guard against such heavy involvement. One church we know of gives its new members a list of ministries and asks them to check the one they'd like to be involved in. But bold letters across the top of the form encourage members to "do one thing, and do it well." Leaders explain that they refuse to be enablers to "volunteer junkies." I once heard the pastor explain the policy from the pulpit: "We want you to do your job, then go home and be with your family. Don't come up here looking for something else to do, because we'll just tell you you've done your job and send you back home."

Great idea.

But unfortunately, very few churches have such limits built into the system. Most will not only let you do all you can possibly handle but unwittingly encourage overload. As a recovering "volunteer junkie," I know it's so. And in the midst of the busyness it's easy to lose perspective—to lose sight of the very reason for our work.

Jesus Our Example

Slowing down to gain perspective is more than just a good idea, it's a biblical one. Jesus often took time out of his ministry to be alone to think and pray.

Luke records an instance when Jesus had healed a man with leprosy and soon found himself surrounded by people needing help. But in the middle of the busyness, he took time to be alone: "The news about him spread all the more, so that crowds of people came to hear him and to be healed of their sicknesses. But Jesus often withdrew to lonely places and prayed" (Luke 5:15-16).

After he fed the five thousand by the Sea of Galilee, people began to realize that Jesus was indeed the Savior they had been waiting for. But instead of getting caught up in the excitement, he quietly disappeared: "Jesus, knowing that they intended to come and make him king by force, withdrew again to a mountain by himself" (John 6:15).

Jesus slowed down often. He always kept his life and goals in perspective. And he encourages us to keep our lives in perspective as well.

While staying at the home of Martha and Mary, he found a

quiet, attentive listener in Mary. Martha, meanwhile, was busy doing what most of us would be doing—buzzing around the kitchen making sure that everything was ready for dinner. There were pies to bake and vegetables to cook and bread to fix and dishes to wash . . . and Martha was intent on seeing that it all got done perfectly and on time. All the while Mary sat comfortably at the feet of Jesus, listening to him talk.

"Lord, don't you care that my sister has left me to do the work by myself?" Martha asked. "Tell her to help me!"

The response Jesus gave would serve as good advice for most of us: "Martha, Martha, . . . you are worried and upset about many things, but only one thing is needed. Mary has chosen what is better, and it will not be taken away from her" (see Luke 10:38-42).

It's amazing how often we get so caught up in keeping the church running, seeing that all the tasks and projects are completed, that we forget to do the one thing that Christ wants us to do—stop, sit and listen!

Halftime Frenzy
I didn't play football during my college days, but I spent every home game mingling with the players on the sidelines. As photographer for the school newspaper, I was issued a press pass that gave me the best, most exciting seat in the house.

Games are intense no matter where you sit, but when you're standing right in the middle of the action you sometimes wonder if your heart will survive the excitement. I was even run over by a few receivers in the end zone a few times while trying to get the perfect, prizewinning picture.

There were times I prayed that halftime would come soon to give me a chance to rest. During one of those halftimes I learned an invaluable lesson about pulling back from the action to gain perspective.

The highlight of every halftime break was when the band took to the field. Having seen them march onto the field playing the school song time after time, I often wondered how they could elicit such excitement from the student body while performing the same program week after week. They would march and play in formation, obviously spelling out some message for the audience, and without fail the crowd would burst into screams and applause as the message took shape. *What are they spelling that can bring the crowd to their feet every week?* I wondered.

So one time as the band took to the field, I made my way up to the top of the bleachers. There I saw what all the excitement was about. The halftime show was made up of a series of messages to the student body, each one tailored to that particular game. As they marched onto the field, the big bold letters "ACU" spelled out the school abbreviation, but as soon as they hit the fifty-yard line, the band members quickly scrambled and came together again in the form of another word. During their fifteen-minute show they spelled out the coach's names, the names of several key players, the score they predicted for the game, the school's win-lose average, anything they could think of to get the crowd excited. And it always worked. With each new formation the crowd went wild.

Since I had spent every halftime show on the sidelines, I'd never realized that the program was different from week to week. From ground level it always looked like the same show. I knew the band was spelling something, but I could never make out what it was.

The same thing happens to us when it comes to church conflict. We spend so much time on the playing field, trying to be right where the action is, that we forget to back away and get some perspective. We forget that sometimes, if we want to know what's really happening, we need to make our way to some high place where we can get a broader view, a quiet place far from the action and excitement.

Now It's Your Turn

If you're feeling the pains of conflict—feeling exhausted and overwhelmed—I encourage you to do what we did. Take some time to back away and reflect. For us two weeks seemed sufficient, but you may feel the need to take more—or less—time. You might consider using the time to go camping or take the family on a vacation. Go visit relatives you haven't seen. Or simply retreat into your own home and relax for a few days.

The location and amount of time aren't as important as what you do with them. Use this time to clear your hearts and minds of any anger, remorse or resentment. Don't think about the conflicts at church or the people who have caused strife. Instead, read a good book. Better yet, read from the Bible—the Psalms may be particularly helpful.

Also use this time for prayer. Ask God to guide your thoughts as you look for insight. Ask him to help you as you take some time to gain perspective—to help you think clearly and lovingly as you reassess your spiritual priorities.

Which brings us to step two of the six-step plan for survival . . .

6

STEP TWO: REASSESS YOUR PRIORITIES, PART 1

*M*ost of us feel pretty certain of what we believe when it comes to church doctrines. We could readily express to others our theology of the church's creeds and teachings—the function of the church, the symbolism of Communion, women's roles in the church, the meaning of baptism, works of the Holy Spirit, the way to salvation and so on.

These are the types of issues that separate one church from another—the positions that define who we are and what we do as a church body. And our own beliefs on such matters help us find a church in which we can feel comfortable.

But few of us, I think, have actually tested our beliefs. Could you defend your positions with any success against those who believe otherwise? Have you taken the time to hold your doctrines and creeds up to the light of Scripture to make sure they are sound? Or have you simply accepted what you've been told by your parents, teachers and pastors?

It's possible, if you are feeling conflict and discontent within your church family, that God is putting those feelings in your heart. God often uses feelings of dissatisfaction and discontent as a means of getting our attention, to tell us that something in our lives may need changing. And if he *is* putting those feelings in your heart about the church you attend, maybe he is trying to tell you it's time for a change—either in you or in your church.

Maybe not. But don't automatically rule out the possibility.

If I were in a church that was in serious conflict with God's desire and will, I believe he would be concerned enough for my spiritual well-being to put some kind of burr in my saddle—an experience, conversation or feeling that would stimulate me to reevaluate my spiritual priorities and beliefs.

I am convinced that God would do something to get my attention—and that he would do the same for any of his children. And I hope that I am always willing to listen when he tries to tell me something.

A Time for Reevaluation

After backing away from our involvement in church long enough to regroup, Ruthie and I decided it was time to do some reevaluating. One of the first things we discussed was the possibility that God was trying to tell us something, to get our attention. As hard as it seemed at the time, we were—and are—committed to listening when God might be speaking to us. So we started asking some tough but important questions about ourselves, our beliefs and our church.

The next few pages will list some of the more important questions we felt compelled to deal with. This is a no-holds-barred list of perspective questions, designed to address the issues squarely. I offer them not because they are somehow all-inclusive or inspired, but to help you get some perspective on your practices and beliefs. They will give you a good place to start as you reassess your spiritual priorities.

Questions of Foundations
As you think about your church, it makes sense to begin with some very basic questions.

1. What first brought me to this church or denomination? When you're trying to figure out where you are, you start by asking yourself how you got there—retracing your steps, so to speak.

What brought you to your church? If you've been in a particular congregation or denomination all your life, maybe it was your parents. Maybe you were led to Jesus by a friend or relative who attended that church. Or maybe you just felt that you needed to go to church, found one close to your home and started attending.

Though some people go through a long time of personal study and prayer before settling on a church home, the fact is that most people find a church based on taste, convenience and enjoyment: Do we like the service? Does the music appeal to us? Is there a good children's program? Is the pastor sincere and likable? Are there people our age, and with similar interests, whom we can get to know? Are there programs and ministries that meet our needs? Does our family seem to fit in?

Though none of these criteria are wrong in and of themselves, they don't address the deeper issue of what church is all about. Great programs and good friends are important aspects of a vibrant church, but they are not enough.

During my college days I once went with a friend to a church that seemed to have everything going for it. When we walked into the door, the place was buzzing with activity. The musicians played well, the people were excited, and the pastor was as polished as they come. But through it all I could tell something was not quite right. It somehow seemed shallow and vague. Though I admit it was only a feeling, it was a very strong and undeniable one.

"How long have you been coming here?" I asked my friend.

"About a year now," he answered, smiling.

"So I guess you must really enjoy it."

"Yeah, it's a great church. About once a month they bring in a new band to play during the services. And our college class has a great time in our Sunday-night get-togethers." He went on for quite a while describing the many fun activities going on in the church.

I was glad my friend had found a church he was excited about, but I still wondered if his reasons for joining the church weren't a bit shallow. So I asked him about some of the core teachings and doctrines.

"Actually, I'm not sure," he answered. "It hasn't really come up. I've been planning on visiting with the pastor about that, but I haven't taken the time yet."

Needless to say, I wasn't impressed.

In his first letter to Timothy, Paul said, "Watch your life and doctrine closely. Persevere in them" (1 Timothy 4:16).

A vibrant church does put a good deal of time and energy into creating a positive atmosphere to attract outsiders, but when growth and entertainment overshadow spiritual depth, when you've spent so much energy making the church fun that you've forgotten what to teach people once you get them there, you have a problem. George Barna calls such churches "a mile long and an inch deep."

Church is, above all else, a place for spiritual growth. A place where we can develop a deeper, more meaningful relationship with Christ. A place where we can encourage and teach one another and build solid, loving friendships. A place where following God's call takes precedence over all else.

Chances are you've not joined a church based on shallow criteria, but still it is important to define what it is that brought you to your church in the first place. If you've never taken the time to take a serious look at where your church stands on issues that are near to the heart of Christ, maybe now is a good time to do that.

2. *What are my church's core beliefs and doctrines?* I'll never forget sitting in a Sunday-school class years ago while the teacher explained some of the doctrines regarding the death, burial and resurrection of Christ. He spent a good deal of time explaining how Jesus actually became sin on the cross so that we might live, and all the while one of the younger women sat listening with her mouth wide open. Finally she burst out, "We don't believe *that*, do we?"

"Yes, I'm afraid we do," the lecturer answered with a tentative smile.

It is never a bad idea to learn all we can about what our church holds true and sacred. Especially if we're in the process of reevaluating our spiritual priorities.

What does your church teach and believe about Christ and the Christian life? Which Christian teachings does it hold as certain? What are the undeniable, unchanging truths of Scripture that it would refuse to compromise on? What core doctrines and theologies define what your church believes and practices?

The Christian faith involves a number of nonnegotiable beliefs. Those of us who recite one of the ancient creeds together each week—the Nicene Creed or the Apostles' Creed—are reviewing those basic teachings. Scripture is also quite clear on a number of moral teachings, summarized most succinctly in the Ten Commandments.

But organized religion has always had a way of adding human traditions and rituals to God's revelation. Traditions can be valuable and healthy, but too often the lines become blurred between the human-made rituals and the God-ordained ones.

Most of us would agree that when we take the Lord's Supper, we are carrying on a tradition established by Jesus just before his death. We are communing with God in a very special, ordained manner.

When we put on Christ in baptism, we are obeying another of God's commands from the Scriptures. We come under the water not because some human being thought it would be a good idea, but because the inspired Word of God calls us to follow Christ in this way.

But alongside these traditions we practice many others that have little or no basis in Scripture. We have Sunday-school classes each week, we sing from hymnbooks or overhead projectors, we plan our worship services and print each program in a bulletin, we have a twenty-minute sermon followed by an altar call . . .

There is nothing wrong with these traditions, in and of themselves, as long as they are kept in perspective. But when churches start placing the same weight on human-made rituals as they do the commands of God, something's wrong.

Jesus gave stern warning against elevating human traditions above God's commands:

Isaiah was right when he prophesied about you hypocrites; as it is written:

"These people honor me with their lips,
but their hearts are far from me.
They worship me in vain;
their teachings are but rules taught by men."

You have let go of the commands of God and are holding on to the traditions of men. (Mark 7:6-8)

It's helpful to step back regularly and take a hard look at our spiritual priorities, to make sure we haven't obscured the gospel with some of our own opinions and traditions. And we need to evaluate whether our church has kept its priorities straight as well.

If you have some doubt as to where your church stands on certain issues, write your questions down. It may be that you need to meet with the elders or leaders to find out exactly what the church believes and teaches about some important issues.

3. How do these doctrines and practices hold up under the scrutiny of God's Word? Once you've clarified for yourself where your church stands on doctrinal issues, the next, most obvious step is to hold those beliefs up to the light of Scripture—to fill the tire with air and see if it leaks.

This may seem like quite a challenge. Most of us are not biblical scholars. We've spent most of our church life depending on those with degrees in Greek and theology to delve into the Scriptures and then share with us what they've learned. And we wonder if we are qualified to question those interpretations.

I think we need to give ourselves—and God—more credit than that. Scripture was never intended to be a confusing set of books written for a highly educated elite. It was written to you and me—to everyday Christians who want to know and obey God.

Paul encouraged Timothy to be diligent in studying the Scriptures: "But as for you, continue in what you have learned and have become convinced of, because you know those from whom you learned it, and how from infancy you have known the holy Scriptures, which are able to make you wise for salvation through faith in Christ Jesus" (2 Timothy 3:14-15).

Luke praised the Bereans for being willing to examine Paul's teachings carefully: "Now the Bereans were of more noble character than the Thessalonians, for they received the message with great eagerness and examined the Scriptures every day to see if what Paul said was true" (Acts 17:11).

Understanding and following God's will is clearly our own responsibility. Every Christian is personally called to test the teachings and doctrines of those in leadership positions (see

Matthew 7:15; 1 Timothy 6:3-5; 2 Peter 2:1-4).

Our abdication of that responsibility is a serious oversight in the eyes of God. When we entrust ourselves without reserve to the scriptural insight of another man or woman, we are, in effect, letting them do our spiritual thinking for us. That's not a risk any of us should be willing to take.

God promised to reveal himself to those who sincerely seek him and his truth: "Acknowledge the God of your father, and serve him with wholehearted devotion and with a willing mind, for the LORD searches every heart and understands every motive behind the thoughts. If you seek him, he will be found by you" (1 Chronicles 28:9).

During this step in your process of reevaluation, I encourage you to immerse yourself in prayer and study. Checking your core beliefs and your church's doctrines and practices against the teachings of Scripture is a crucial step toward understanding God's call on you.

I am convinced that God would not want any of his children involved with a church that distorts or diminishes the truths of Scripture. And I believe one tool he would use to reveal the errors would be a feeling of disunity and discomfort.

I need to stress here that this may or may not be the case in your church. Not all churches in conflict are struggling because they have strayed from God's revelation in Scripture. But it is a possibility we need to be willing to consider. As we reassess our spiritual priorities, we can trust Scripture to shine a light on those areas where we might be wrong and also to reaffirm those beliefs and practices that are in harmony with God's revelation.

Questions of Nurture
Next let's turn to issues of spiritual growth.

4. Does my church foster spiritual growth and encouragement, working to draw people into a deeper relationship with Christ? An old country church in the South displayed a sign above the front door, perhaps hung there by one of the members. It read: "I know I ain't what I oughta be, and I hope I ain't what I'm gonna be, but at least I ain't what I used to be."

By definition the Christian life involves growth and forward motion. Is your church one that helps propel your spiritual growth—one that exhibits the qualities described by Paul in Ephesians?

Consequently, you are no longer foreigners and aliens, but fellow citizens with God's people and members of God's household, built on the foundation of the apostles and proph-ets, with Christ Jesus himself as the chief cornerstone. In him the whole building is joined together and rises to become a holy temple in the Lord. And in him you too are being built together to become a dwelling in which God lives by his Spirit. (Ephesians 2:19-22)

A church devoted to being God's dwelling will always see the spiritual health of its people as its first priority. Its leaders will be consistently working at encouraging and equipping God's flock.

And effective church leaders will know the importance of encouraging personal study and prayer over blind obedience. I like the way author and lecturer Rubel Shelly describes the church's role in equipping the saints:

The church of Jesus Christ must challenge people to make their faith personal. Every congregation of believers needs to be a place that not only allows but encourages people to ask questions and investigate for themselves. The goal of good teachers is not to spoon feed theology but to give people the tools and methods for getting into Scripture for themselves.[1]

5. *Does my church serve as a partner with me in the spiritual nurturing of my children?* I recently visited with a children's pastor from a large church in Washington. She was bursting with excitement as she explained some of the wonderful things God was accom-

plishing through her church's ministry to children: "A few years ago we built a large children's church wing on the back of the building to help house all the kids in our growing Sunday-morning program. And right now we're using every square inch of that wing. The kids just keep coming, and we just keep trying to expand to fit them all in."

She went on to review the many sacrifices the church had made over the years to accommodate the children's program: "The church has grown so much that we've long since outgrown our building. We're holding three services every Sunday and are considering starting a fourth. We desperately need a larger sanctuary.

"Still, just last week we held a congregational meeting to discuss our need for a new auditorium, but the congregation voted instead to put the money toward another expansion to the children's wing for additional classrooms. It's wonderful being in a church that puts so much stock in the training and nurturing of children."

It's not hard to see why this church has experienced such rapid growth. Any congregation that is willing to put significant energy into ministering to kids will easily gain the loyalty of its members—as well as others who are in search of a home congregation.

Lee Strobel, in his book *Inside the Mind of Unchurched Harry and Mary,* makes this observation about the expectations of today's parents:

Regardless of the level of Unchurched Harry's spiritual interest, despite his own dissatisfaction with the church, what draws him back is his feeling many times that his children need some religious training. . . .

If Unchurched Harry and Mary see a youth program that's relevant, dynamic, and staffed by people who have an authentic faith, they're going to be more likely to explore what adult programs the church provides.

I know two parents who are coming to our church only because their six-year-old son enjoys the youth ministry so much. "About Wednesday or Thursday, he starts asking if we're going to church on Sunday," the mother said. "He doesn't stop until I tell him yes." While he's with kids in his age group, the parents are in the adult service, and they're starting to grow spiritually.[2]

Jesus held a special place in his heart for children: "Let the little children come to me, and do not hinder them, for the kingdom of heaven belongs to such as these" (Matthew 19:14). And he makes it clear that he expects the same attitude in us. "Whoever welcomes a little child like this in my name welcomes me. But if anyone causes one of these little ones who believe in me to sin, it would be better for him to have a large millstone hung around his neck and to be drowned in the depths of the sea" (Matthew 18:5-6).

A pastor in my city is known to say, "It is a sin to bore a child with the gospel." I agree with him. It's heartbreaking to see churches spending money and time on elaborate computer systems and fresh new songbooks while the children's teachers go week after week in need of new materials. When I see Sunday-school teachers scrambling for the copy machine five minutes before class—copying pages from an out-of-print coloring book to keep the kids busy—it's all I can do to keep from crying.

What will become of the church if we lose sight of our children? Who will capture the hearts and minds of the next generation if the church abdicates that responsibility?

If you are in a church that doesn't make children a priority, if your kids are being bored with the gospel week after week, you may have some serious soul-searching to do. And perhaps some church-searching as well.

But don't make that decision yet. Not until you've finished

your evaluation process. And certainly not until you've consulted the Lord and spent time in listening prayer.

Step three of the plan is designed for that purpose. But first there are some more tough questions to ask—questions about vision, character, spiritual gifts and relationships.

7

REASSESS
YOUR
PRIORITIES,
PART 2

We recently visited a church that is known throughout Colorado Springs for its commitment to outreach. As we drove into the parking lot, we noticed a sign on the front of the building that read: "Without vision, the people will perish."

At the top of the brochure the greeters handed us at the front door was a simple statement of vision: "Helping You Reach Your World." That theme ran through every aspect of their ministry. The Christian education curriculum, from children's to adults' classes, aimed to equip people for this vision. And the theme ran through much of what was said by the pastor during the sermon.

This church holds three services on Sunday mornings to accommodate the members' different styles and preferences of worship. One follows the seeker-service model pioneered by Willow Creek Community Church in South Barrington, Illinois. Regardless of which one you attend, you find out quickly that the church is serious about its vision for outreach.

The result: At this writing, the church has grown from around 650 members to over 1,300 in just eighteen months. The weekend before we visited, the bulletin recorded over 1,600 people in attendance. While meeting people during the time of fellowship, we had trouble finding someone who wasn't also a visitor.

George Barna, known as an expert on trends in the American evangelical community, has spent years researching growing, vibrant churches. In his book *The Power of Vision* he makes a powerful statement about the kind of church people flock to:

In evaluating churches that are growing and healthy as compared to those that are stagnant or in decline, one of the key distinctions that emerges is the existence of true vision for ministry.

In every one of the growing, healthy churches I have studied, a discernible link has been forged between the spiritual and numerical growth of those congregations and the existence, articulation and widespread ownership of God's vision for ministry by the leaders and participants of the church. Conversely, visionless congregations fail to experience spiritual and numerical growth. Rarely in my research do I find such overt, black-and-white relationships.[1]

If personal and spiritual growth is important to you and your family, then consider question six in your reevaluation process.

Questions of Vision

Individuals need vision. So do churches. The next few questions are designed to help you think carefully about the vision and direction of your church.

6. Does my church have a clearly articulated vision that drives its purpose and ministry? In his seminars, motivational speaker Zig Ziglar uses an illustration to show the importance of setting clear goals. "I have only shot a bow and arrow a few times in my life," he begins. "But I will guarantee you that today I could out shoot the world's best archery marksman. I'd bet any amount of money on the contest. Provided, of course, that I could be granted one small stipulation. Before his turn, he must be blindfolded and spun around in a circle several times."

Little or nothing is accomplished without clear, well-thought-out goals—as well as a definite plan of action for reaching those goals.

Many churches, like people, spend their lives floundering from one day to the next, going one direction for a while, then changing their course and heading in another. Someone in leadership has an idea one day to focus on the homeless. So he starts getting people interested, and before long a blanket and food drive has begun. For a time people are caught up in the excitement, and a feeling of unity and common purpose ensues. But because the project is not connected to a clear goal—a greater vision and purpose—the interest soon dies down and the drives end.

A few months later someone comes up with another idea. "Let's start a ministry to singles," she says. So the church shifts gears and heads in that direction—only to find that interest soon wanes once again. The ministry dies, and the church coasts until the next bright idea comes up.

Several serious problems arise when churches lack clear vision.

☐ *Without a clear direction, churches never get anywhere.* The story is told of an airplane lost over the ocean in the middle of a hurricane. The captain decided it was time to inform the passengers of their dilemma, so he turned on the intercom. "I have some good news and some bad news," he began. "The bad news is that we've lost our guidance system and have no way of knowing where we are or which way we are going. The good news is, we're making great time!"

The problem with not knowing where you are going is that you never get anywhere that you need to be. There's no ultimate point to your trip.

☐ *It's impossible to keep people working toward a goal when you have no goal to work toward.* Any sales executive will tell you how futile it is to try and produce growth and excitement in a sales team when there is no stated, specific goal for each day. The key ingredient of a successful season in sales is a regular incentive program set before the sales force. Long-range goals are broken down into a series of short-term objectives, and people are constantly being reminded of the rewards they will reap if they can reach these goals.

I'm certainly not trying to equate life in Christ with good sales techniques. But churches need to understand the psychology of vision. Without motivation, without clear long-term and short-term goals, a congregation will accomplish little if anything for the kingdom of God.

☐ *Without a goal to focus on, people will focus on themselves.* It's often called "navel-gazing." When people have no purpose, no reason to focus outward, they begin to focus inward. It tends to breed selfishness and tunnel vision.

Ask judges how lawbreakers are best rehabilitated, and they will inevitably cite community service. When we're helping others—focused on the needs and feelings of others instead of our own desires—we're happier and more content. And we're growing spiritually and emotionally as well.

☐ *Lack of vision produces disunity.* Author Max Lucado tells of a fishing trip he took as a boy with his father and his best friend. They arrived in the evening, set up tent and went to bed dreaming of all the fish they were going to catch the next morning. But when they woke, they found that the weather had turned ugly. It was cold and rainy, so they spent the day in the tent playing board games.

That night they went to bed hoping that the weather would change, but it didn't. Again they were forced to spend the entire day in the tent. But by this time they were starting to get on each other's nerves.

By the third day the weather still hadn't cleared, and cabin fever kicked into high gear. They stopped even pretending that they liked each other, explains Lucado. So they loaded their gear into the car and went home.

He sums up the moral to the story in one short, powerful sentence: "When people who are called to fish don't fish, they fight."

The ultimate vision of every healthy church is to reach as many people for Christ as possible—to be "fishers of men." When we lose sight of that vision, we lose patience with each other.

If the members of your church seem to be in constant conflict with one another, perhaps the problem lies in a basic lack of vision. Maybe everyone is fighting because no one is fishing.

7. If the church does have a clear vision, how was that vision arrived at? When businesses develop vision statements, they do it by weighing a lot of different factors. What does the customer want? How will customers' needs and wishes affect the marketing of the product? What do the surveys say? How much cash can we generate with this vision? Everything hinges on the bottom line, and anything legal that will help toward that end is considered as a possible means.

But churches must take a different approach. The church was never intended to be a tool for "selling Jesus." When we get into that line of thinking, we lose sight of our true purpose.

If God has a vision for every Christian (and I believe he does), then he also has a vision for every church within his kingdom. As his people we need to be striving to discover that purpose— both individually and collectively.

A good example of a church with vision is the Willow Creek

Community Church. The detailed statement of Willow Creek's vision is summarized in this phrase: "To turn irreligious people into fully devoted followers of Jesus Christ." The leaders discerned the church's strengths and weaknesses and decided to target the unchurched.

People at the Eastside Foursquare Church in Kirkland, Washington, asked themselves the same questions and found that their church body was strong in different areas. As a result they came up with a different vision statement: their primary focus as "reaching nominal Christians," who they define as "those who claim to be born again, but are not committed to any church."[2]

Whatever the vision of your church, it's important to put on paper your intent as a church body. It helps focus and remind the members of the goal they share in Christ.

But even more important is seeing that your vision aligns with God's will for your church. A vision must be his before it becomes ours.

No church will ever serve the Lord effectively unless it involves the Lord in every step of the process. No matter how visionary the leaders, no matter how attractive the marketing, no matter how committed the people, unless the vision was arrived at through prayer, fasting and meditation on God's Word, the outcome will be futile. Psalm 127:1 says, "Unless the LORD builds the house, its builders labor in vain."

A church that does not pray may see growth in numbers, may look vibrant and on track, may even be unified in purpose, but if the people have set out on their own—if their vision was arrived at through human wisdom—they will never be able to draw others closer to the Lord. And that is the ultimate purpose of any church.

I like the way George Barna puts it:

Christian leaders must recognize that any vision based upon their own capacities will be flawed and limited. Because they are sinful individuals with restricted capacities and selfish tendencies, relying upon their own intuition, skills, talents, insights and dreams is dangerous, especially when the objective is to determine how to conduct effective ministry.

Authentic Christian leaders are people who know that when they are left alone to make decisions, those choices invariably reflect their unregenerate nature. In other words, their choices demonstrate values, beliefs, desires and goals that are not perfectly aligned with the mind and heart of God. But because they are Christian leaders, they know they must pursue God to gain a better perspective on what they ought to do with the resources and opportunities entrusted to them by God.

When people create a vision that is not God-centered, it may result in temporal progress but [is] unlikely [to] provide a positive, long-lasting impact.[3]

8. Does the vision of the church align with my vision for my faith and my family? If you are satisfied that your church has a clear vision and purpose, and that those in leadership articulated this vision after an intense search into God's will, you have but one more concern regarding the matter: Does the vision of the church fit with what you believe is God's will for you and your family?

I've heard someone say that churches with vision are like buses. If you're wanting to know where a bus is heading, you look at the sign on the front. If it reads "New York City" in big, bold letters and New York is where you want to go, you know at a glance what bus to board. But if your goal is to get to Los Angeles, you have two options: you can get on the bus and make the trip uncomfortable and annoying for your fellow passengers by complaining that it's going in the wrong direction, or you can find a bus that's going to Los Angeles. Everyone will be happier if you do the latter.

Churches are not buses—I know that. I don't mean to trivialize the issue with this analogy. But it is a practical way to look at the situation. A church cannot be everything to everyone. It cannot be at once both traditional and progressive. It cannot travel in two different directions at the same time.

A visionary church has set a clear vision and purpose—it is headed in a distinct direction—and some will not agree with this vision. Different preferences and ideas create differing agendas. And differing agendas within the same church body create conflicts.

A good friend was recently telling me about some of the struggles she was having in her church. "The leaders are really great," she said. "They have been very up-front in telling people what plans they have for the future of our church. They're wanting to create a church that is appealing to unchurched young couples. They're working hard at making the services more contemporary, and we're putting more time and energy into the children's program than we ever have. I'm thrilled with the vision they've set for us."

"So what's the problem?" I asked her. "It sounds as if things are going in your direction."

"Oh, *I'm* very happy with the direction of the church," she assured me. "The problem is with a handful of members who are making things miserable for everyone. They know how the elders feel, and they know which direction the church is heading. But they are very vocal about their disapproval, and they're doing all they can to jeopardize any changes we try to make. One of these men came to a church meeting recently and sat arguing with anyone who brought up a new idea. After someone reminded him that the vast majority of the people in the church were in favor of a more progressive service, he crossed his arms, tightened his jaw and said, 'I don't care who wants it; as long as I'm around it's not going to happen. And I'm not leaving!' "

As a result of these few unhappy travelers, the church is feeling the pangs of disunity and division. Its leaders are having to work overtime at putting out small fires—even though a very large percentage of the people are thrilled with the new vision they've set for the church.

If I were in a church that was going in one direction and I wanted to be going in another, I hope I would be willing to either change my plans and be happy with it or find another church home. Because I follow Christ, I am responsible to deal with the issue on my own—quietly and peacefully.

Scripture is very clear on how God feels about a divisive person. Proverbs 6:16-19 lists six things that God hates, and among them is "a man who stirs up dissension among brothers." When Paul listed the acts of the sinful nature, among them were "discord," "dissensions" and "factions" (see Galatians 5:19-20). And writing to Titus, Paul was very clear about Christians' need to guard against divisive and arguing attitudes: "But avoid foolish controversies and genealogies and arguments and quarrels about the law, because these are unprofitable and useless. Warn a divisive person once, and then warn him a second time. After that, have nothing to do with him. You may be sure that such a man is warped and sinful; he is self-condemned" (Titus 3:9-11).

Is your church going where you want to go? Is the vision of the leaders one that you can share? If not, can you realistically—and effectively—change your plans and make the best of it?

These are tough but important questions that each of us needs to answer. If we are unhappy, if we are disgruntled, if we are in disagreement with the vision of the leaders, we have several options. But none of the options allow for a divisive attitude and manner. There is no justification in the eyes of God for a person to cause disunity in the body of Christ.

Questions of Character
Next it's important to take a look at who leads the church and

what sorts of people they are.

9. *Is the pastor of my church a godly person, committed to the truths of Scripture?* Jerrien Gunnink writes of a preacher he calls George whose self-serving attitude did harm to every congregation he served:

> George began his ministry in a small church in a farming community of Iowa. Usually a new minister tries to please people, but George found himself in deep trouble after two years. It seems that George took offense to any constructive criticism from his parishioners. He was defensive and lectured his parishioners about their faults. It was apparent that any suggestion made to George found its way into next Sunday's sermon by way of rebuttal. These conditions were the makings of a strife-torn church, and after four years George was dismissed.
>
> The scenario was repeated in George's next charge. At this writing he is in his third pastorate, and antagonism is already building.[4]

Pastoring a church is a high calling, demanding great sensitivity, compassion and spiritual insight. When ministers become so self-involved that they don't even see the harm they are doing to others through their poor attitudes, they leave a trail of hurting people in their wake.

People depend on their pastors and elders. In times of distress, many laypeople turn first to their pastor. When people need wise counsel, they hope the pastor of their church can help. And if the pastor is not there for them, not sensitive to their struggles, not understanding of their needs, they can easily lose their faith in the church—even their faith in God.

I have a minister friend who preaches for a small congregation in the South. He has been with the church for many years. In spite of his long experience, he is still quite awkward in the pulpit. To put it bluntly, he is often rather boring. In spite of this,

the church loves him and wouldn't dream of letting him go—
because any skill he lacks in the pulpit is more than made up for
in his ability to pastor the flock. He is warm, compassionate and
sincere. When someone is hurting, when someone needs prayers
or a listening ear, they know he is always there. And his advice is
sound and godly.

Too many church leaders today are skilled in public speaking
but greatly lacking when it comes to personal relationships. The
bigger the crowd, the brighter they shine. But one on one they
seem cold and distant. If I had to make a choice, I'd sit at the
feet of the somewhat boring yet godly preacher any day.

Another aspect of a faithful minister is commitment to the
integrity of Scripture and courage to tackle the tough truths of
the Christian faith head-on, regardless of the consequences. Too
many preachers over the years have chosen denominational
loyalty over personal and biblical honesty. They have held to the
party line even on issues where they felt their denomination was
mistaken. In many cases they simply steered clear of the awkward
passages that didn't seem to fit with current thinking in their
church.

But over the last few years I've noticed an encouraging trend:
pastors of all denominations are speaking out on many of the
inconsistencies of the past. Pastors and preachers are no longer
compromising themselves to keep peace in the pews and hang
on to their jobs. In fact, I could readily name a dozen good
ministers who have lost their jobs over the last few years because
they were no longer willing to keep silent on some controversial
issues.

It's ironic, of course, that ministers of the gospel would lose
their jobs for preaching the truth. But it's encouraging nonethe-
less that they were willing to do so.

When Ruthie and I were part of a church going through deep
conflict, we thanked God many times for our pastor, Jack. More

than any preacher I've known, Jack showed himself willing to preach the hard truths—to examine the inconsistencies in his movement and tackle the issues head-on. I watched in amazement over the years as he openly questioned the church's sacred cows, encouraging others to examine the Scriptures for themselves and correct him if he was wrong. Needless to say, he's come under a great deal of fire over the years. I saw more than a few hand grenades lobbed his direction. But always he was committed to the truth, committed to searching the Scriptures and bringing that truth forward to his flock.

I often think of Jack as I reflect on Paul's words to Timothy:

I give you this charge: Preach the Word; be prepared in season and out of season; correct, rebuke and encourage—with great patience and careful instruction. For the time will come when men will not put up with sound doctrine. Instead, to suit their own desires, they will gather around them a great number of teachers to say what their itching ears want to hear. They will turn their ears away from the truth and turn aside to myths. But you, keep your head in all situations, endure hardship, do the work of an evangelist, discharge all the duties of your ministry. (2 Timothy 4:1-5)

Is your minister committed to the truths of Scripture, pastoring the flock with honesty and sensitivity, or does he or she simply tell people what their "itching ears want to hear"?

10. Do I trust and respect the leaders and teachers of the church? The story is told of a young army recruit serving his first day on the frontlines of battle. As the fighting heated up and the bombs started landing closer and closer to his foxhole, he climbed out and ran away as fast as he could. He had run quite a distance before he was stopped by an officer carrying a service revolver. "Stop right there, private, or I'll see that you get a formal court-martial and execution!" the officer shouted.

The private trembled with fear. "Please don't shoot, Captain.

Give me another chance!"

"All right, private," he answered. "I'll give you one more chance. But it's Colonel, not Captain."

To this the young private replied, "I'm sorry, sir. I didn't realize I was that far back!"

Not all armies keep their officers far from the lines of battle. But those that do usually have little success. It is said that one of General George Patton's greatest strengths was his ability to inspire loyalty among his troops. He won that loyalty by his willingness to walk arm-in-arm with his men into the heat of battle—to lead by example.

Winston Churchill also was known to be outspokenly critical of leaders who used their rank to keep themselves safe from harm, away from the action. In the heat of a war, he regularly spent time on the frontlines of battle.

Too many church leaders fail to see the wisdom in leadership through camaraderie. And too many church members view their elders and teachers as high-ranking officers who watch the war from afar.

Effective leaders and elders know the harm in this kind of thinking. They know that people will never remain loyal to a group of people who spend long hours behind closed doors, making decisions with little sense of the commitments and concerns of the congregation. Churches need leaders who are willing to stay in close contact with the members. Leaders who know intimately the needs and desires of the flock and who care deeply for each individual member.

In *A Church for the 21st Century* Leith Anderson outlines some important qualities of effective church leaders:

☐ *Attuned to the culture.* "It is not enough to know the Bible," Anderson writes. "We must also know our culture and our people. We must have incarnational ministries in the pattern of Jesus."

☐ *Flexible.* Leaders must be able and willing to adapt to new and different ideas.

☐ *Relational.* Churches need leaders who are approachable and real, who "live where their people live."

☐ *Good communicators.* Leaders need to be able to communicate a vision and move others to take ownership of that vision.

☐ *Entrepreneurs.* Leaders should have the ability to drive churches and ideas toward success. As Anderson writes, such leaders "see the opportunities in the changes and strategize to turn those opportunities into good for God's kingdom and Christ's church."

☐ *Risk takers.* Healthy leaders are willing to fail in order to succeed. They do not shy away from risk simply to protect their safety and security.[5]

Just giving people a leadership title or office does not make them leaders. Leaders act as leaders whether they have the title or not.

I know a man in a very large church who holds no official title or position. But he is clearly a leader, with a large and loyal following. He does not use this fact to throw his weight around; in fact, he is quite modest and humble. But when he speaks, people listen. Even—sometimes especially—those who hold the official positions of leadership.

Barna says more about this type of leader:

We have to make a distinction between someone who holds the position of leader and an individual who behaves as a leader. Many churches are led by individuals who hold a leadership post or title. What truly identifies people as leaders, though, is not their title but their mind-set and actions. Similarly, a common characteristic of all true leaders is that they have vision. A godly leader is one who operates from a base of God's vision for his or her ministry.[6]

Do you trust and respect the leaders and teachers of your

church? Are they men and women who have gained your loyalty through godly lives and service to others? Are they in tune with God's vision for them and their church? Do you trust them with the souls of your family and friends?

Of the ten questions I've posed thus far, this one may well hold the top position in spiritual importance. A church can function with many faults, but if the leaders are ungodly and self-serving, if they are more interested in power and position than in the souls of needy people, if they have no burden to grow in knowledge of the Lord and godly wisdom, then the church is in dire need of help. I would run from such a church.

On the flip side of that coin, if a church is led by godly, spiritual men and women who want more than anything to do the will of God, you can bet that God will hear their prayers. Any church, no matter how embroiled in conflict, no matter how deep in a struggle for survival, will eventually find its way to peace if the leaders are committed to seeking peace.

8

REASSESS YOUR PRIORITIES, PART 3

*T*ony Campolo tells of a time he was invited to speak at a small country church in Indiana. He arrived early in the morning to find an elderly man wandering about the sanctuary, making sure everything was ready for the service. He checked the thermostat and made sure the windows were opened just the right amount. Then he went up and down each aisle to make sure all the hymnbooks and Bibles were neat and in place.

"You must be the custodian," Campolo remarked.

"No," he answered, "I'm just exercising a special gift of the Spirit."

Campolo, intrigued, asked him exactly what gift of the Spirit he believed God had given him.

"The gift of helps," he answered proudly. "Check it out in 1 Corinthians 12:28. You'll find it there. Paul talks about the gift of helps."

So Campolo looked it up, and sure enough, the old man was right: "And in the church God has appointed first of all apostles, second prophets, third teachers, then workers of miracles, also those having gifts of healing, those able to help others, those with gifts of administration, and those speaking in different kinds of tongues."

The man went on, "You know, we get a whole parade of preachers coming through here on their way to bigger and better things. Each of them stays for a few years and then moves on. Each of them thinks he's the best thing that this church has ever seen, and each of them thinks he's going to put this church on the map. Well, after they're gone for a few years we have a hard time even remembering their names."

Then, pointing to himself, he continued with a grin, "One of these days ole Harry's goin' to die, and the people of this church won't know what hit them. They'll come to church the next Sunday and find that nobody turned up the heat. They'll find out the hard way who shoveled the snow on all those winter days. And they'll take forever to figure out where half the stuff they need to run this church is stored away."[1]

Questions of Gifts and Unity
Harry knew exactly what gift he had, and he was proud to use it. I know a few people who have similar gifts, and the church would indeed be in sad shape without them.

And that leads us to question eleven in the church reevaluation process.

11. Do I know my spiritual gifts? And is my church a place where I can effectively use those gifts to minister to others? Wes, a good friend of mine, is a professional musician. He plays in a western band, has recorded several albums and CDs, and has written some beautiful ballads. You'd be hard pressed to find a more gifted singer and performer.

Yet until a few months ago Wes attended a conservative church with a long-standing tradition of noninstrumental worship. They sang only a cappella music and were not open to having solos or special music during worship. Congregational singing was the only accepted form of music during Sunday-morning services.

Wes stayed in the church out of a feeling of obligation to his wife, his friends and God. Though he didn't feel God leading his family elsewhere, he did feel that his God-given talents were going to waste. "I know this sounds selfish," he confided to me once, "but I really do wish I could use my talents at church. Week after week I go to church and sing, but I never feel like I'm glorifying God in the ways I could be. Actually I feel like I'm quenching the Spirit, and I sometimes wonder if it's not a sin to do that."

What frustrated Wes most was that many of his brothers and sisters in the church truly couldn't understand why he felt the way he did—why it was such a burden for him to keep his talents to himself. They knew he enjoyed music but didn't understand how it could mean so much to him. No one could fathom how hard it must be for him to sit week after week with his hands folded in his lap.

My experience has been different. As editor of our church's newsletter and head of its publications ministry, I was able to use my gifts for our church on a regular basis. I wonder what it would have been like for me if my church had no use for such things—if the leaders had no use for newsletters or pamphlets or bulletins or directories. Of course I would have found places where I could help, but it would have been painful to have my church ignore a gift that is quite important in my life.

How would you feel if the one thing you enjoy doing above all else—the foremost talent that God has given you—was seen in the church as a hobby useful only for personal gratification? I'm afraid I probably wouldn't be as gracious as Wes was.

Several months ago Wes and his family felt strongly that God was leading them to another congregation. A progressive church in their area was looking for some people to help lead its music ministry—a need that fit perfectly with Wes's passion. Within two weeks of the family's first visit, the church put Wes's talents to work. He was asked to join the worship team that played during services, and soon afterward he was recruited to lead singing for the youth classes. It was clear to Wes and his wife that God had led them to this church.

I visited Wes's church a few weeks ago and sat in as he sang some of the songs he had written to the large high-school class. Many of the young adults were moved to tears as they listened. And Wes seemed happier than I had seen him in years. He has found his place.

Not all churches are set up to make use of the talents of every member. Of course there must be some eccentric or unusual talents that simply could not fit in. But I can honestly think of very few.

A church that includes a good mechanic can encourage him or her to minister to people in the church and the community who can't afford oil changes and brake adjustments. People who are good at handling hammer and nails would be invaluable to a church's community-service project. A baker or cook could help organize a Thanksgiving dinner for the poor.

Here is a question that the leaders of any church would do well to ask: "What could be accomplished for the Lord if we used the talents and resources available in this body?" Such a church will make a greater impact on its community than they ever dreamed possible. If all churches took this question seriously, the world would be changed forever.

Does your church work to help all of its members define their spiritual gifts? And once the gifts are defined, does the church work at helping them use their gifts in ministry to others?

12. Does my church promote a spirit of unity, or does it unwittingly foster a mood of disunity? Congregations, like people, have very distinctive personalities. If you've had the chance to visit different congregations and sit in on worship services as an outsider, you've no doubt become well aware of this. Each church has its own disposition and style. Some churches are kind and benevolent. Others are angry and rude. Still others are riddled with indifference.

Though individually the members of these churches no doubt have their own traits and mannerisms, collectively they exude a very clear *group* attitude and personality. The spirit of the group as a whole is easily discernible.

Our family recently attended a special event at a nearby church. We arrived early and found some good seats near the front. As members of the congregation filed in and found their seats, I had a strange sense of a collective personality taking shape.

The worship leader sat at a grand piano to the right of the stage, playing quiet, melodic tunes. The room was warm and cozy, and a mellow, soothing sensation filled the air. The design of the building added to the feeling of calm. The carpet was plush and earth-toned, while the walls were rich with dark wood and flagstone brick. A couch and some comfortable chairs made the stage area homey. There was no pulpit, only a microphone on a stand in the center of the stage. A large brick fireplace stood on the right side of the stage.

When the minister spoke, his tone was more conversational than lecturing. The mellow feeling carried through the entire service.

This description may give the impression that the church was passionless and boring, but that wasn't the case at all. Being there was actually rather exhilarating. The church communicated a spirit of family—of unity and love.

The mood of the service was akin to the way I might feel on a getaway retreat in the mountains in a large, secluded lodge, sitting around the fire with a handful of my best friends while someone softly played the piano. In fact, before I knew it I was completely caught up in the congregation's feeling of calm. Instead of analyzing the mood as an outsider, I was just feeling it. I was part of the group. It was delightful.

Another church we visited recently was completely different. As we walked into the auditorium, excitement filled the air. The music was loud and upbeat, and when the worship team began singing, congregants jumped up and stayed on their feet for the entire song service, clapping their hands and tapping their feet the whole time.

A few minutes into the sermon, a commotion started at the back of the auditorium; the back doors burst open as a drama team rushed down the aisles to center stage. Everyone was laughing and craning their neck to see what was going on. The team performed a short skit pertaining to the day's topic, then ran back down the aisles and out the back door.

This church too had a very distinctive personality—one of excitement and enthusiasm. Yet unity and love were felt just as strongly as in the church I described earlier. Though the styles and moods were as different as night and day, the two churches had an important thing in common—the people were one in purpose and spirit. And each time I found myself completely caught up in the spirit of oneness.

I don't know all the dynamics at work when a church reaches this type of harmony, but I do know that once the people find it, the feeling is powerful and undeniable. You can sense it in the air.

Is your church a unified church? Do the leaders work at promoting oneness—a feeling of common goals and purpose? Is your church's personality marked by love and understanding or bitterness and arrogance?

The next time you are sitting in a worship service, try to see your church from the eyes of an outsider. Would a visitor feel at home in your church? Would he or she be drawn into a spirit of unity or turned off by a sense of disunity?

Questions of Relationships

These questions will probably lead you to think about relationships in your church—to the outside community and among members.

13. Does my church encourage physical and spiritual outreach? In chapter seven I quoted the vision statement of the Willow Creek Community Church: "To turn irreligious people into fully devoted followers of Jesus Christ."

Though not all churches share that mission statement, all churches do have an obligation and mandate to reach out to the lost and hurting. And any church that ignores that responsibility should not expect God's blessings on its ministry.

One of the church's functions as Christ's body is to reach out to the world with his message of hope and compassion. We are to demonstrate God's mercy and grace to a world that knows little about such concepts. And a church that doesn't reach out to the world, that doesn't help the poor and hurting, that doesn't minister to the lost of its community is missing out on the main reason for its existence.

Christ left little doubt as to what he expects from his people. What we've come to know as the Great Commission is a command Christians and churches must never overlook: "Go and make disciples of all nations, baptizing them in the name of the Father and of the Son and of the Holy Spirit, and teaching them to obey everything I have commanded you" (Matthew 28:19-20).

In what is perhaps the most sobering passage of all Scripture, Jesus clearly defines the fate of those who call themselves Christians but don't work to help feed and clothe the helpless and needy:

> Then he will say to those on his left, "Depart from me, you who are cursed, into the eternal fire prepared for the devil and his angels. For I was hungry and you gave me nothing to eat, I was thirsty and you gave me nothing to drink, I was a stranger and you did not invite me in, I needed clothes and you did not clothe me, I was sick and in prison and you did not look after me."
>
> They also will answer, "Lord, when did we see you hungry or thirsty or a stranger or needing clothes or sick or in prison, and did not help you?"
>
> He will reply, "I tell you the truth, whatever you did not do for one of the least of these, you did not do for me."
>
> Then they will go away to eternal punishment, but the righteous to eternal life. (Matthew 25:41-46)

Some years ago, when we lived in Texas, we became involved in the Highland Church in Abilene. Over the years Highland had gained a reputation in the community as a caring, compassionate church that was committed to reaching out to the poor and needy.

Using a dozen buses, we would pick up hundreds of unchurched kids every Sunday morning and bring them to church. Though it was a costly ministry, complicated to run, the entire church was committed to its success. A food and clothing center was set up to help the poor—no questions asked. And the church held regular drives to keep the center stocked and ready to serve.

A few years ago a handful of the church's members dreamed of giving Christmas to families who would otherwise go without. So they rallied volunteers, gathered financial support and threw a party to end all parties. The first year over four hundred people were fed. Clothes and blankets were distributed to each family, and every kid went home with a new toy. The ministry has grown each year since then.

Out of this same Christmas ministry came an idea for helping families of lower-income schools in the area. The church has since adopted two schools, both in poverty-stricken areas of town. Food and clothing banks are set up on the school grounds, and doctors from the church make regular visits to give free exams and treatment to children of poor and broken homes.

It's wonderful to see how God has blessed this church for its efforts.

We found it deeply moving to watch a church do what churches are supposed to do. No drug can give you the kind of high you get when you're a part of something so right, so compassionate, so near to the heart of God.

Take a look at the priorities and programs of your church. Is it reaching out to the lost, the poor, the sick, the cold and the imprisoned?

14. Do I have a close-knit group of friends at my church—friends who have a positive spiritual and emotional influence on me and my family? Once at a Bible study the leader asked each person to voice his or her prayer needs. The usual requests were being made, until he came to a young woman I had known for some time. Tears came to her eyes as she asked for the group's prayers. "I've been praying for a long time that God would provide us with some close Christian friendships," she began. "We have a lot of friends in our church now, but they are all surface-level friendships. We don't have anyone we feel really close to on a spiritual and emotional level."

Her request surprised me. I had always seen her as juggling more relationships than she could handle—sort of a "relationship junkie." She was regularly having lunch or dinner with friends. Yet here she was in tears, lamenting the fact that none of these friendships were close and fulfilling.

Every one of us needs at least one good friend. Someone we can openly share our joys and struggles with. Someone who understands us and loves us in spite of our shortcomings.

Ruthie and I are blessed to have a close circle of friends at our church, friends we can relate to on many levels. For as long as I can remember, Ruthie has been praying that the Lord would lead us and our kids into healthy friendships, and God has clearly provided that for us. Just this morning I had breakfast with three men friends from our church. It was a wonderful, spiritually uplifting way to start the day. We talked about our struggles as Christians and fathers, shared some ways God has been working in our lives and encouraged each other toward a deeper, more meaningful relationship with God. It is like that every time I get together with this group of friends. Our breakfast and lunch times together make me a better husband, father and Christian.

The writer of Proverbs knew what he was talking about when he said, "As iron sharpens iron, so one man sharpens another" (27:17). Spending time with men who are committed to God and family always makes me feel "sharper" and more attuned to God's will.

Our get-togethers often remind me of the admonition to Christians in the book of Hebrews: "Let us consider how we may spur one another on toward love and good deeds. Let us not give up meeting together, as some are in the habit of doing, but let us encourage one another—and all the more as you see the Day approaching" (10:24-25).

I thank God for these godly friendships.

It's encouraging to see churches developing programs and ministries that are meant to bring people together. Over the last few decades the trend has been toward larger churches, and now these large churches are seeing the need to "feel" smaller. So they are implementing small group ministries, women's ministries and men's ministries. In our church we've found that as a wide range of small groups have developed, the whole congregation has gained a sense of being more unified.

So take a good look at the personal relationships you have within your church family. Do you have a core group of close friends who love Jesus? Do you have relationships built on mutual love and respect and trust? Do your friends spur you on toward love and good deeds? Can you share your joys and struggles with them? Do they hold you accountable and work at helping you keep your faith strong and your integrity intact?

I need those kinds of friends. All of us do. May God make you rich with the relationships you need.

So . . . What Now?

That completes my list of perspective questions. Unless, of course, your church scored well on every aspect of the test, in which case I have one more question for you: What are you doing still reading this book?

If you are feeling the stress of a church in conflict, though, you probably are looking at a significant number of negative answers. Very few churches in the midst of conflict will fare very well under such a fine microscope. In fact, my questions may have succeeded in making your church look worse than it really is. A crooked stick always looks more crooked when you lay it beside a straight one.

But we need to remember that churches are like people—none of them are ever perfect. God doesn't expect it, and neither should we. Churches are made up of people—sinful people. The leaders will not always lead as well as we'd like, the ministries will not always minister to us, the preacher will not always speak our language, the music will not always match our tastes.

If you're looking for a perfect church, stop looking. Because it doesn't exist.

But we *can* expect church to be a place where we feel comfortable. A place where we can worship God with others of like mind. A place where we can bring our friends and feel good about the impression it will make. A place where we can grow spiritually and emotionally, and where we feel the Spirit of God working in our lives.

If your church needs to be better, needs to be more of a partner with you in your spiritual growth than a barrier to it, don't be afraid to admit that fact. If your church needs to be more in the center of God's will, needs to pray more, minister more, fight less, don't deny those shortcomings. Don't be afraid to call such things into question—to "test the spirits to see whether they are from God" (1 John 4:1).

Until this point, that's what the focus of this book has been—to put our churches through a process of reevaluation. You've taken a good, hard look at where your church is in relation to where it should be. And you've held its teachings and practices up to the light of Scripture.

But if you're looking for a way to tally the final score and see if your church passed the test, I'm afraid I can't help you. Even if I had developed such a score sheet, I'd be hesitant to share it. Only God has the authority to judge your church. And only God can know what's best for you and your family. This plan for surviving church conflict isn't meant to give you those kinds of answers, only to point you in the direction of God's guidance and direction.

What I hope you've gained so far is a sense of perspective—a better sense of how you feel about your church and your family's spiritual health in the midst of the conflict. You've backed away from your situation far enough to gain a better view, and you've considered what you need—and what God expects—from a church body. These are two crucial first steps to take while looking for God's guidance.

At this point in the process, if the struggles of your church have created a heavy burden on your heart, there are two options to consider: either God wants you to find a new church home, or he wants you to recommit yourself to your present church and work at becoming a peacemaker. There are no other viable choices.

Step three in the plan is designed to help pinpoint which of these two choices is God's call for you. Does he want you to go, or does he want you to stay?

There is a way to know. If we ask, and if we listen, he will take us down the right path.

9

STEP
THREE:
GO TO
YOUR
KNEES

*C*harles Stanley once wrote:

God desires to make known the unknown to His children. He desires to unveil the hidden. Yet many times we are satisfied not knowing. Either we aren't willing to take the time to wait, or we aren't sure God even wants us to know. . . .

We are to call, we are to expect an answer, and we are to know the unknown.[1]

Knowing the unknown is precisely what we need when we're trying to find God's will. I've often wished God would open up the heavens and send down a hand to write on the walls of my office when I'm in need of guidance. So far it hasn't happened.

A friend once told me she heard God speaking to her in an audible voice while she was driving in her car. I wanted to ask if she might have an electrical short in her radio, but I just nodded my head and smiled. I won't discount her experience, but nothing like that has happened to me either—and I don't expect it ever will.

Still, I know God communicates with me. I've experienced it too many times to believe otherwise.

When Ruthie and I moved to Colorado Springs six years ago, it was very clear to us that God was leading the way. I had built a small but growing business in Texas and had no reason to want to leave. But God put an undeniable sense in both of our hearts that we should move. We knew the sense was from God, but we didn't know why or where he wanted us to go.

As a step of faith, we sold our business and trusted the Lord to show us his will. Ruthie thought we should consider Portland, Oregon, and I had my heart set on Connecticut. But when we looked into those two possibilities, doors started slamming shut in front of us. It was clear that God was leading us elsewhere.

We somehow sensed that he might be wanting us in Colorado Springs, so we drove up one day to investigate. It still seems a blur how quickly the doors started opening for us. Within hours of our arrival to the city, we were sitting across the table from a realtor, signing a lease agreement on a house. We had looked for neither a realtor nor a house. We had simply gone to dinner and decided to visit a church before settling into a hotel for the night. But God clearly had other plans for us.

Today, six years later, we can see why God wanted us here. We've made some personal and professional contacts that would have never come our way otherwise. And God has used my writing ministry in ways that I never would have dreamed. This is exactly where God wants us at this time in our lives—that is clear to us.

Prayer Brings Perspective
When I am working on a writing project, Ruthie and I spend a

great deal of time in prayer, asking God's guidance and wisdom. More than anything, I want what I write to be accurate and in tune with the truths of Scripture. I pray that God will lead me in my words and show me where I might be in the wrong.

When those prayers are sincere—and I hope they always are—he does not let me down. More times than I care to admit, God has put people and circumstances in my path that have shown me error in my opinions and positions.

One very powerful example of this came during a recent trip to visit family and friends over the holidays. During a conversation with a man I've known most of my life, we began discussing this book project. The topic of church conflict brought up some things that had been going on in his church. Though he and I shared many views on what churches should and shouldn't be, I could tell that we didn't agree on how churches should go about reaching that goal.

As we talked, it became painfully clear to me how cold and uncaring some of my ideas sounded. Though I had spent considerable time researching the topic of church growth and renewal, I had not put much thought into how people could be hurt by my ideas. I believe so strongly in the need for churches to be culturally relevant in order to reach lost people that I tend to get single-minded and tunnel-visioned. I don't always think of the people who would be threatened and run off by my aggressive agendas.

My friend, on the other hand, is a kind, caring soul with a heart the size of Texas. And in his gentle way he began reminding me of my shortsightedness.

Sitting in my friend's living room, I felt a very strong sense that God was telling me to listen to him. "You need to hear this," the Spirit was telling me. So I stopped talking and started listening.

For two hours I sat as my friend spoke. Though he didn't know it, he was bringing down my sacred cows one at a time with his words. The Lord was speaking to me through him—that one thing I know for certain. And since that day I've been forced to look at myself and my views through a different set of lenses. I no longer try to force my views and agendas on others. I'm more understanding of other points of view. In fact, I'm a better man—and this is a better book—because of my friend's insight.

Such experiences don't happen to me that often. It is only when I put time and energy into praying for guidance and then sincerely wait and watch for an answer that I feel the Spirit's leading.

Listening for God's Voice

I can relate to a story Charles Stanley tells about a time when he felt the hand of God touching and leading him:

> As I was praying one afternoon in 1967, I began feeling as if God had something very specific to say to me. The more I prayed, the more the burden increased. I mentioned this to my wife, and we decided to take our vacation early and spend the time seeking God's guidance. We went to the mountains of North Carolina for two weeks, intent on finding out what God was saying to me.
>
> Annie and I spent the majority of our time fasting and praying. We waited, expecting God to follow up the burden with an answer. . . .
>
> Then one afternoon soon afterward, I was on my face before the Lord and the veil lifted. God wanted me to start a school. I hesitated to commit myself to such a task, but God made it clear to me that His instructions were to be obeyed, not just considered. He unveiled the hidden to me when I called on Him to do so; He showed me the things I knew not of.[2]

There are many ways God chooses to communicate his will to us.

I've felt strong directives from God while reading Scripture. Many times God has convicted me of a sin that I needed to deal with through a paragraph in a book that I just happened to pick up, or through some words in a message from the pulpit on Sunday morning. I've often felt God's hand shaping me through the daily experiences of life.

But there are times when God speaks to us in other ways. When we choose to quietly, earnestly listen for God's will, we can hear him clearly through the "still, small voice" that whispers in our souls.

Psalm 46:10 says, "Be still, and know that I am God."

It is when we back away from the noise, close our eyes and open our minds that the Spirit speaks the loudest.

I like the way Bill Hybels describes it:

God's power is available to us when we come to him in solitude, when we learn how to focus and center our hearts and be quiet before him. When we learn the discipline of stillness before God, we find that his leadings come through to us clearly, with little interference. . . .

Whatever you ask the Lord, you will be amazed at the way he leads. Once you are quiet and tender before him, waiting to hear him speak, he will bring a verse to mind or will guide you through your thoughts and feelings. As you build the discipline of stillness into your life, you will find these quiet moments in God's presence becoming incredibly precious to you.[3]

Throughout Scripture we are told to stop and listen for the voice of God:

Listen and hear my voice;

pay attention and hear what I say. (Isaiah 28:23)

Whether you turn to the right or to the left, your ears will hear a voice behind you, saying, "This is the way; walk in it." (Isaiah 30:21)

I will instruct you and teach you in the way you should go;

I will counsel you and watch over you. (Psalm 32:8)

God's promises are not to be taken lightly. When we ask and listen for his voice, he speaks.

Be Prepared to Follow

You've been spending a lot of time in reflection and reevaluation. You've backed away from your situation far enough to gain perspective and have taken an objective, in-depth look at where your church is in relation to God's will and your needs. In fact, you've been preparing to take your concerns before God, and now it is time to do that.

This is not a trivial matter. If we want to know God's will, one of the prerequisites is that we be willing to follow wherever he might lead. At times that can mean our lives will be disrupted in a big way. But if we are committed to obedience, we're concerned for more than our own convenience and comfort. We must be willing to *act* on God's will once he has revealed it to us.

At times I have prayed for guidance and then felt the Lord leading me in a certain direction, but instead of following I closed my ears and took things back into my own hands. When I responded that way, I sinned. And I often felt the consequences—both subtle and severe.

Ruthie told me of a time she believed she squelched the voice of the Spirit. It has bothered her ever since.

Our family has grown over the last few years, and last summer we considered moving into a larger home. The local housing market was on the upswing, and we wondered if it was a good time to look, but after praying about the situation we felt God would help us find a house to suit our needs if that was his will. So we started house-hunting.

During the first few weeks of looking, it was clear that the houses we were viewing were quite overpriced, both for the market and for our budget. But then we found a home that seemed too good to be true. The price was well under what we'd expected to spend, yet the house was bigger and more attractive than we'd thought we would find. It was no mansion, but it was well suited to our needs. I wanted to make an offer on the spot, but Ruthie had reservations. "We haven't been looking very long," she said. "And I was hoping to find a house farther north."

I didn't understand, but decided to go along with her instincts. The next day the house sold to another couple.

Ruthie was very upset that we had lost the house. Later she told me that while we were walking through the house she had a strong sense that the Spirit was telling her to suppress her reservations. "You need to submit to Frank on this," she sensed the voice saying in her soul. But she closed her mind and didn't listen.

After that, doors started closing for us in our search for a house. You would think that in a city of 300,000 people, we'd be able to find another house that would meet our needs and budget, but we simply could not find one. After four months of looking we felt very certain that the Lord was telling us to stay put and make do with the home we had.

The Danger of Turning a Deaf Ear

Had we listened to the voice of the Spirit when he led us to the house meant for us, we would now have plenty of room for our family and the company we entertain each winter as they come to visit. Instead we are feeling the consequences of our unwillingness to listen. Since that time housing prices have skyrocketed, so we are sitting tight, waiting for them to come down and level out before we renew our search.

The Lord opened a small window of opportunity for us, and we chose not to go through it. Now we are feeling the consequences. And though I can certainly think of worse consequences to bear, the lesson we learned was a very powerful one—disobedience to the Spirit is never a good idea.

If you are going to pray that God guide you regarding your church situation, it is important that you are clear on the possibilities ahead. Are you truly willing to leave if that is where God leads? Even if it means having to cut some old ties and relationships and work at developing new ones? Are you willing to stay in your present church and become an agent of peace if that is what God wants from you? Even if that means repenting of your past attitudes and laying to rest some long-standing hurts and resentments?

Are you willing to follow wherever he may lead, regardless of your particular wants and wishes?

Before praying, search your heart for that willingness. As Bill Hybels writes:

> The . . . reason we may not hear God's voice is that we don't plan to do anything about it. God speaks, we listen and nod and say, "How interesting!" But if we don't follow up on the Holy Spirit's leadings, he may see no reason to continue speaking. . . .
>
> Some of the most important decisions in my life have made no sense at all from a worldly perspective. But I have learned that I can't afford not to respond to his leadings. So if God tells you to do something, do it! Trust him! Take the risk![4]

A Time to Pray

As you bring your concerns before the Lord, it helps to know specifically why you are praying and what you are praying for. Since you've spent so much time reassessing your beliefs and reevaluating your church, at this point you should have a very clear picture of what your prayers should focus on.

When Ruthie and I were in the midst of church conflict and praying for guidance, we knew exactly what was causing our feelings of discontent. There were many things that delighted us in our church. But we saw some problems that were of great concern to us—enough, at least, to warrant a serious reevaluation of our involvement.

Almost all of our concerns revolved around the fragmentation we felt due to differences of opinions. Those differences, we believed, were caused by a basic lack of clear vision. Many people had ideas about which direction the church should be taking, but no one, it seemed, was willing to take a stand and set a clear path.

So we knew what to pray for. We prayed for guidance for our family but also for the leadership of our church. "Lord, you know what direction our church needs to go," we prayed. "And you know who in the church is capable of leading it toward that vision. Please take the reins and guide our church toward that vision. Raise up a leader to do your will. And show us where we fit into that vision. If we are to stay and work toward change, guide us in that direction. If we are to move on, please let us know that and give us the courage to do so. Whatever your will, we commit ourselves to obeying and following."

Your situation may be different. Perhaps your concerns are caused by other areas of conflict. Maybe you question the motives of your pastor. Maybe you are uncomfortable with some of your church's doctrines and teachings. Maybe you are concerned about a lack of spiritual depth in the church. Maybe your friends have been dragging you down instead of helping you grow. Whatever your concern, bring it before the Lord. Specifically and often.

God may choose to do several things in response to these kinds of prayers.

☐ *He may change the situation.* God may choose to work in your church through your prayers—lifting up a leader, working in the heart of the pastor, convicting some teachers of wrong doctrines or guiding you to the friendships you need. There is no situation in the world that God can't change.

☐ *He may direct you to stay, giving you the grace to endure and come through the conflict a changed person.* God's "shot of adrenaline" is a powerful thing. He may choose to use you as an agent of change, as a mighty force in his plans to bring direction and unity to a strife-torn church.

☐ *He may confirm that he has plans for you in another church.* Our God is not a God of stagnation. He is a potter, continually molding and shaping his precious creations. And change is a natural part of that process. Following God is a daily adventure. When God is leading and we are following, the road may not always be comfortable, but it will be far from boring.

If God has another church in mind for you, he will lead you in that direction. And when he does, hold on tight and be prepared for excitement!

Where He Leads I'll Follow

God has a plan for each of our lives, and he desires to reveal that plan to us. If we are feeling the need to ask for his guidance, there is a reason for those feelings. In the words of Lloyd John Ogilvie, "Prayer starts with God. It is His idea. The desire to pray is the result of God's greater desire to talk with us. He has something to say when we feel the urge to pray. . . . He, not us, was the author of the longing for His help."[5]

Whatever plans God has in mind for you, rest assured that he will lead the way and watch over you as you follow. There is no safer, more exhilarating place to be than in the loving hands of a mighty God.

10

STEP FOUR: IF YOU'VE DECIDED TO STAY . . .

A turning point in our church struggles came one Sunday morning. We had been praying earnestly for guidance and direction and were actively looking for an answer to those prayers. But on this particular day, looking for God's guidance was the furthest thing from my mind.

It was one of those mornings when nothing seems to go right. We woke up late and arrived at church hurried and frazzled. The kids were particularly squirmy and active, and since I had missed breakfast, my stomach was growling before the service even began. My attitude was not great.

But during the song service I felt a strange calm coming over me. The stress of the morning started to fade away, and a tranquillity began to take shape in my soul.

As we sang I looked around the auditorium at the many familiar faces. For the first time in several months, I felt a sense of unity with the congregation. I felt a part of things. I felt like I was with family.

There was nothing particularly moving or eventful about the service that morning. In fact, it was rather ordinary. It wasn't the emotion of the music that carried me. But the feeling was very real and powerful.

As I looked around the room, I noticed the many people with whom we had built good relationships—our friends in the faith: my weekend golfing buddies, the people who worked with me on our newsletter, friends from our small group. I felt a bond that I hadn't felt for some time—even with those who I knew to have strong differences of opinion with me.

I felt that the Spirit was speaking to me. Still, I wasn't sure.

During the next few weeks several things happened to confirm my feelings. Over lunch with a good friend I learned of some new and exciting programs being planned for the children's Sunday-morning classes. One of my complaints had been the lack of clear focus I'd seen in that ministry.

A few days later I learned that the church was planning some special events and film series aimed at reaching the unchurched of our community. Again, a lack of outreach had been among my concerns.

Several other instances like that happened over the next few weeks. Ruthie and I both believed that the Spirit was speaking to us. And we felt that the message was clear: God wanted us to stay and help our church go forward. We were in a position to help the church move through the conflicts, to help bring peace to the body. God wanted to use us during this difficult time of turmoil. So we decided we needed to stay.

Interestingly enough, until this time I was fairly sure we would be moving on. The conflict that our church had undergone—

mostly before the split—had been so emotionally draining that I had become rather cynical. Too much had happened. I didn't know if I could honestly be happy in this church again. Though my prayers were sincere, I had drifted into thinking that I knew the answer before God even spoke. But I was wrong. God softened my heart and calmed my spirit.

And so, to my surprise, we decided to stay.

A Time for Renewal
Maybe you sense that God is telling you to stay with your church family as well. After spending time reassessing your spiritual priorities, then praying for guidance, you've felt the Lord telling you not to give up on your church—to stay and work toward peace and unity and love.

If so, it is time to look forward—to forget the past. This is a time for renewal. A time for rebuilding. A time for recommitment. *And* a time for some more reevaluation.

The Lord has called you to stay for a reason. And the fact that you are not changing churches doesn't mean changes are not in order. In fact, it's quite likely that changes are needed. If you've been struggling to get along, if you've been unhappy, if you've felt the need to consider moving to another church, there is probably a need to rethink your involvement habits and practices. Maybe you need to rethink your friendships. And maybe you need to rethink your attitudes and opinions.

Ruthie and I felt that God was leading us to stay in our church family, but we didn't want to simply fall back into the same patterns as before. We knew the dangers of doing that. If we were unhappy then, what would keep us from being unhappy in the future? So we did some soul-searching—some more reevaluation. We decided it was time to look at our church and ourselves in a different light—to seek personal and spiritual renewal.

A Time to Look Forward

Leonard Sweet once said, "The future is not something we enter. The future is something we create."[1]

I'll never forget a wonderful lunch I had with a new friend from our church. It was during the period that Ruthie and I had been praying for guidance, and on this particular day I was feeling rather cynical about the future of our church. But my friend didn't share my pessimism.

Throughout the lunch he talked about the many positive aspects of our church, in spite of the conflicts. He reminded me of the people who make up the core of the congregation and how united they were in wanting to help the church move forward. He spoke of the renewed vision coming from the leaders. He pointed out how fortunate we were to have such a competent and godly staff of ministers. "We are positioned to be a powerful, history-making church," he said. "If we could only get together and move forward, instead of dwelling on the past, we could change the world!"

What a remarkable attitude he had. His message was something I needed to hear. That's why the Lord put him in my path.

Our God doesn't look back, and neither should his people. He wants us to look forward, to set aside the past, to be visionaries for the kingdom. Just as he forgave our sins and promised to remember them no more, we need to be willing to forgive our church for its shortcomings, leave behind the pain from the past and move forward with renewed determination.

Remember the words of Paul: "But one thing I do: Forgetting what is behind and straining toward what is ahead, I press on toward the goal to win the prize for which God has called me heavenward in Christ Jesus" (Philippians 3:13-14).

A Time for Rebuilding

This is also a time for rebuilding, for bandaging old wounds and patching broken bridges. The worst thing about conflict in the church is that it usually leaves relationships shattered and strained. Even when solutions are found, we may have a hard time forgiving those we've differed with.

I know two women who attend the same church but haven't spoken in years. As they pass each other in the halls, neither looks in the direction of the other.

Years ago they had a sharp disagreement over some doctrinal issues. Neither could understand the position of the other. Their conflict grew with every encounter, and soon they were both writing letters to the church leaders demanding that the other be confronted and corrected. The elders stepped in and mediated the dispute, then encouraged the women to forgive and forget. But even though they've dropped the issue, they've yet to rebuild their friendship.

Though these two women are both liked by many in the church and considered kind and considerate people, they can't seem to put their differences aside and accept each other as friends.

Jesus made it very clear what he expects from us when we've had differences with others: "If you forgive men when they sin against you, your heavenly Father will also forgive you. But if you do not forgive men their sins, your Father will not forgive your sins" (Matthew 6:14-15).

If some of your relationships have been strained by the conflict in your church, I encourage you take the first step in rebuilding the broken bridges. It's time to set aside your differences and learn to value people as God values them.

A Time for Recommitment

I once heard someone describe the difference between *involvement* and *commitment*. "It's like when you order bacon and eggs for breakfast," he began. "You know that the chicken is involved in the process, but the pig—he's committed!"

Most of us are involved in the work of our local church, but how many of us are truly committed to it? How many of us are willing to go beyond helping the church with its ministries and instead set aside our personal wants and desires for the good of the group? How many of us are committed to unity, to peace, to becoming a part of the solution when conflicts arise instead of being another log on the fire of discontent?

Many church conflicts can be traced to a basic lack of commitment among members. People want to be involved, but they don't want to commit themselves to the church, to be devoted to the vision of the church regardless of the personal inconvenience they may suffer. When people are more interested in what they can get out of church than they are in what they can add to it, churches begin to feel strife.

Luke paints a beautiful picture of what a church can be like when everyone works together for the good of the whole—when we commit ourselves to one another for the cause of Christ:

They devoted themselves to the apostles' teaching and to the fellowship, to the breaking of bread and to prayer. Everyone was filled with awe, and many wonders and miraculous signs were done by the apostles. All the believers were together and had everything in common. Selling their possessions and goods, they gave to anyone as he had need. Every day they continued to meet together in the temple courts. They broke bread in their homes and ate together with glad and sincere hearts, praising God and enjoying the favor of all the people. And the Lord added to their number daily those who were being saved. (Acts 2:42-47)

That's what happens when Christians commit themselves to each other. When they work through their differences and focus instead on the common bond they have in Jesus.

If you've lost the zeal and commitment you once had for your church—or if you never really committed yourself at all—now is a time to devote yourself, heart and soul, to the people and leaders who make up your church family.

First, *recommit to your leaders*. It may be that you need to publicly repent of your past attitudes. If you've been a divisive force in the conflict your church has suffered, if you've openly criticized the leaders, if you've been an agent of discord instead of a messenger of peace, then maybe some apologies are in order.

Second, *recommit to your friends*. Let those close to you know that you are now investing in the future of the church and that you plan to do whatever needs to be done to keep your relationships there strong and intact. Let them know what their friendship means to you, how they have blessed your life in the past and how you hope to see that relationship grow and deepen in the future.

Third, *recommit to your family*. If church conflicts have often found their way into dinner conversations at home, if you've let your problems at church affect the way you treat your family, then let them know of your remorse. Pledge to keep a positive attitude in the future.

Fourth, *recommit to God*. After all is said and done, the person you most need on your side right now is God. Let him know of your sincerity in wanting to change, to move forward, to recommit yourself to your church, your friends, your family and your faith. Only he can help you keep that pledge.

A Time for Reevaluation

I used to enjoy going with friends to a horse ranch outside of town and riding for an hour or so through the countryside. There were trails going every direction from the corral, and we were allowed to take any trail we wanted as long as we were back at a given time.

The first half of the trip was always fun. The horses would go pretty much where we wanted them to go. The pace was leisurely, and we talked as we rode. But everyone dreaded the trip back, because as soon as you turned your horse around and pointed its nose in the direction of the barn, it was all you could do to hang on without losing your grip. Forget about even trying to take a detour. All the horse had on its mind now was getting back to the barn and having lunch with all the other horses.

You would think these overfed, cooped-up horses would be glad for a long hike through the countryside, but instead all they wanted to do was get back into some familiar surroundings where they felt safe and secure.

We're a lot like that, aren't we? Most of us talk about wanting some excitement in our life, wanting to experience new and different things, but when talk comes to do we end up heading back to the barn where it's safe and where we know everyone else. We opt for the familiar over the fresh and exciting.

Though there is nothing wrong with wanting stability, it often leads to stagnation. And stagnation in the church is never a good thing.

Too many of us find ourselves in a rut at church, working at a task or ministry out of a sense of obligation and familiarity. We don't necessarily feel a call to that ministry; we're simply filling a need. Something needed doing and we weren't doing anything else at the time, so we volunteered. And years later we're still doing it.

I would venture that much unhappiness in churches can be traced to people's having no clear picture of their spiritual talents and gifts. They are not especially good at what they're doing (through no fault of their own), but they don't have the heart or the wherewithal to relinquish the task.

I've seen people go year in and year out teaching Sunday-school classes with a frown on their face and no lift in their voice. Among friends they admit that they don't particularly like kids, yet they find themselves surrounded by them week after week.

I've watched men serve as church greeters who don't even know how to begin a conversation. They hand out bulletins and shake hands without ever looking you in the eye. The last thing they want to do is help a visitor find a classroom.

Churches need to plug people into ministries based on their gifts and talents instead of simply placing a warm body in a vacancy. And individual Christians need to put more thought into uncovering their gifts and finding a place where they can minister effectively.

If you've found yourself unhappy in your work at church, maybe it's because you've been working at the wrong jobs. Maybe not. But it is a possibility to consider. Instead of returning to the same projects—heading back to the barn where everything is safe and familiar—why not use this time to reevaluate your church involvement? Ask yourself how you came to serve in your past ministry and whether you feel adequate for the task. Is this something you are good at? Do you enjoy doing it? Would you be more effective elsewhere? What do you feel the Lord calling you to do?

A Time for Renewed Love and Unity

Perhaps the most difficult aspect of trying to move forward in a church that has seen strife and conflict is forgetting the past and working toward a renewed sense of unity. Often when we find ourselves at odds with our brothers and sisters in Christ, it's hard to put the past behind us.

But if churches are to be effective in mirroring Christ to the world, it is crucial that we love each other, that we learn to forgive, that we live and work in harmony with each other.

Jesus said, "By this all men will know that you are my disciples, if you love one another" (John 13:35). And Paul elaborated on the importance of love and unity in the faith: "As God's chosen people, holy and dearly loved, clothe yourselves with compassion, kindness, humility, gentleness and patience. Bear with each other and forgive whatever grievances you may have against one another. Forgive as the Lord forgave you. And over all these virtues put on love, which binds them all together in perfect unity" (Colossians 3:12-14).

There is no virtue in staying with a church family for the sake of mere duty, obligation or martyrdom. Unless we can learn to love and unite with our brothers and sisters in the faith—to resolve the past and move forward with renewed vitality—we are doing no favor to anyone by staying around.

But if we *can* move forward, if we *can* forgive and forget, if we *can* renew our commitment and vision, God will be glorified because of it. The world will know that we are his disciples. And we will find the "perfect unity" that Paul encouraged us to strive for.

I can think of no better way to end this chapter than with some words from author Wynne Gillis. He sums up clearly what it means to love our brothers and sisters.

Love is not deserved; love is. When we love another truly, he does not have to "measure up." We accept and love him as he is. This is the kind of love which Paul says bears all things, believes all things, hopes all things, endures all things (I Cor. 13:7). When we know that we are loved in this way, then and only then can we dare throw our masks into the corner and reveal ourselves. Only in such an atmosphere of love and acceptance can real trust, intimacy and openness flourish and grow.[2]

11

STEP FIVE:
IF YOU'VE
DECIDED
TO GO . . .

Steve was the longtime pastor of a large congregation in Texas. Like many churches, his was starting to feel the strife of differing agendas and philosophies of worship. Steve was among those pushing for change and renewal in the services. Others in the church fought for stability and tradition. The elders were divided on the issue.

Camps started forming, and soon the church was positioned for a head-on battle.

Like any good pastor, Steve worked overtime at keeping the peace. Though he didn't give up his own ideas, he put many of them on the back burner for the sake of unity. But hard as he tried, the war waged on. And it showed little sign of letting up anytime soon.

Steve had been praying fervently for peace and direction. One option he considered was moving on and finding work elsewhere. So he waited anxiously for a word from the Lord.

It was during a father-son camp-out that his answer came to him. One night he was lying in bed praying for guidance when he heard a faint cry coming from his son's room. He quietly slipped into the room and crawled into bed beside his son.

"What's wrong, Eric?" he asked, wiping the tears from the boy's red, swollen cheeks.

"It's nothing, Daddy," Eric answered, still sobbing uncontrollably.

Steve persisted. "Eric, you know you can tell me anything. I really want to help. Please tell me what's wrong."

"I just can't stand it at our church anymore," his boy blurted out. "Everyone is always fighting, and I can't understand why everyone hates you so much there."

Then Steve knew what he needed to do. God's will came through loud and clear. A letter of resignation was written the day he returned from camp, and today he is preaching for a nondenominational church in another part of the city—one that has long since worked through the issues Steve had been dealing with in his previous church.

Some Ground Rules for Leaving

If we are caught in a strife-torn church, there are times when the best thing we can do is move on. And if so, God will usually make that quite clear to us. Chuck Swindoll speaks to that possibility:

> If I can't go on with the way things are in a particular ministry, I need to resign! But in doing so I should not drag people through my unresolved conflicts because I didn't get my way. If separation is the best solution, doing it graciously is essential. If your disagreements are starting to outweigh your agreements, you ought to give strong consideration to pulling out. Who knows? This may be God's way of moving you on to another dimension of ministry.[1]

Over the past months several of my good friends have decided that God was leading them to a different church. It is never an easy thing. At times it's like saying farewell to friends who are moving to another city or state—you say you will keep in touch, but many times you don't, and the relationships are never the same. Other times, because the friendships are stronger, you do keep in touch. Still, you miss seeing your friends' smiling faces on Sunday mornings.

God brings people in and out of our lives often. We can feel glad for our friends who are facing new possibilities, and we need not feel guilty when we are the ones who are called to move on. Nor should we question God's wisdom in calling us. If God has called you to move on, that is what you should do. It won't be easy, but time will heal the wounds.

Before you go, however, there are some ground rules to consider. Though Scripture is relatively silent on what to do when severing church ties, it is full of lessons on how to live graceful and loving lives—even in the midst of conflict.

Rule 1: Leave Quietly

At one church service I attended, an elder surprised everyone by stepping to the pulpit before the closing prayer and reading a letter of resignation. The letter did more than just tell of his plans to resign. It was a cutting indictment of some of the policies and people of the church—including the other elders. For a good five minutes he stood venting his anger and disagreement with the church's leadership and direction. We all sat stunned. No one knew how to respond.

Another man I know of was scheduled to say the closing prayer at his church on the day that he had planned to leave and go elsewhere. Having kept quiet about his plans, he used the prayer as a personal soapbox. It was sprinkled with accusations and criticisms of the church, falling just short of naming names. After he said amen, he folded his paper, tucked it in his pocket and walked out the back door, never to be seen again in that sanctuary.

I've known people who wrote long, biting letters to the church pastors and leaders before taking their membership elsewhere. They no longer wanted to be a part of the church, but they couldn't seem to leave without making sure people knew how angry they were.

I can understand the impulse. When we're disgruntled, the thought of "going out with a bang" is satisfying somehow. We want the last word when we feel we've been wronged. But that doesn't make it right to vent our bitterness. In fact, it is clearly wrong. The Golden Rule tells us to treat others with the same respect that we would expect from them (Matthew 7:12). Jesus tells us to turn the other cheek when we feel someone has wronged us (Matthew 5:39).

The only right way to leave a church is quietly and lovingly. If you must write a letter, emphasize the things that make for unity. Thank the leaders for their dedication to the church and their willingness to serve God and the flock. Let them know that despite your differences you still love and respect them.

Writing that you're leaving because they are a "bunch of idiots who don't know how to lead" may make you feel better at a gut level, but it does nothing but harm—both to you and to the church. On the other hand, leaving on friendly terms, with a kind and loving attitude, brings glory to God. He is always praised when we do what is right instead of indulging our selfish impulses.

Some good friends of ours decided to leave their church several months ago. It was sad news for all their friends in the church, but it was clear that they needed to go. And God has blessed them in their new church home. The dignity and grace they showed when they left was an inspiration. They met with the leaders one at a time to explain their decision. Then they met with the pastor. Each time they thanked the leaders for their friendship and spiritual nurturing through the years. They left with no hard feelings toward anyone. They were the perfect examples of grace in the midst of conflict.

Rule 2: Leave Without Proselytizing

Though I'm sure there are exceptions to this, I've yet to see a church divide where the ones who left didn't begin pressuring their friends to go with them. It's almost inevitable. The thinking is, the greater the number who leave, the more successful the split is (if you can imagine labeling any church split "successful").

That kind of thinking is simply wrong—both in attitude and in practice. Scripture is very clear about the evils of divisiveness:

Hatred stirs up dissension,

but love covers over all wrongs. (Proverbs 10:12)

A perverse man stirs up dissension,

and a gossip separates close friends. (Proverbs 16:28)

I urge you, brothers, to watch out for those who cause divisions and put obstacles in your way that are contrary to the teaching you have learned. Keep away from them. For such people are not serving our Lord Christ, but their own appetites. (Romans 16:17-18)

Warn a divisive person once, and then warn him a second time. After that, have nothing to do with him. You may be sure that such a man is warped and sinful; he is self-condemned. (Titus 3:10-11)

There are some canons that I don't want to find myself on the business end of. And this is clearly one of them!

Whenever I feel God leading me to leave a church body—any church, for any reason—may he give me the grace, love and maturity to leave quietly, discreetly and alone. No words of dissension. No pressure on friends or family. No gossip. No proselytizing. Simply a calm, loving parting of the ways.

Rule 3: Leave Definitively

In every congregation there are people who have gained reputations as "the disgruntled ones." They're always "about to leave." They love the attention they get when they vent their frustrations, always ending their monologue with an attention-getting pronouncement: "I can put up with a lot of things, but this is where I draw the line. If something isn't done about this, I'm just going to leave!"

Then after crying wolf a few dozen times, they add another sentence to their tired speech. "I know I've said this before, but *this time* I really mean it!"

No one takes these people seriously. Not about leaving, and not about anything else. Their effectiveness in the church is diminished through their constant whining. If they ever did leave, people would probably be glad to see them go! And they'd likely be just as unhappy in their new church.

If you are such a person, then my harshest words thus far are meant for you: *get over it!* You're giving everyone a headache.

If you're not, then heed the lesson we've all learned by watching those who are. When you give criticism, make it constructive, loving and well thought out. When you give your opinion, stop and listen to differing points of view. And when you decide to leave, leave! Don't hang around looking for pity and support. And don't give ultimatums—"Either play my way, or I'm going to take my ball and go home!"

Decide what to do, then do it. But until then, be quiet, be cheerful, and be definitive in your words and actions.

Rule 4: Remember to Say Goodby

I credit this rule to my friend Cindy. As I discussed this book with her, she told me of an exodus from her home congregation and how hard it was for everyone involved. "Tell people to remember to say goodby when they leave," she said. "Many of our friends left without saying goodby, and it really hurt. We wondered later how much our friendship really meant to them in the first place."

Cindy's right. As I think back, I remember feeling the same pain and disappointment when some of my friends neglected to say goodby.

When leaving your church home, it's easy to get so involved in your own wants and needs that you forget the feelings of others. You have a hundred things on your mind: What will my parents think? Will we find another church? How do I bow out of my ministry duties? And who will do them once I'm gone? What will the leaders think when they find out we're leaving? The concerns and loose ends we have to tie up can be overwhelming. And in the middle of all the chaos, it's easy to forget our friends, our brothers and sisters in Christ. It's easy to forget to say goodby and explain why we feel that God is leading us elsewhere.

But good friends deserve that much from us. Because even though we will promise to keep in touch, we both know that often—too often—things are never the same.

Still, friendships don't have to die simply because you are changing churches. You're just going to worship at another congregation, you're not moving to Siberia! In fact, let's add another rule to the list just for good measure.

Rule 5: Don't Sever Good Friendships
Once a week Ruthie gets together for a time of prayer and Bible study with some good friends. Only one of the other women attends our church. Yet some of her most precious relationships are in this group.

I have a weekly breakfast get-together with a group of dear friends, some of whom left our church some time ago. We never considered severing our ties of fellowship just because the Lord has led them elsewhere to use their spiritual gifts.

Granted, some friendships will fade when you leave. But the relationships you've built with close friends, spiritual mentors and "blood-brothers" in the faith should never be severed in the process. Work at keeping hard-to-come-by friendships alive and vibrant.

Don't Forget the Kids

And there is one other important matter to address: how do we help our children deal with the pain of leaving? If you have kids over the age of four and under eighteen, it's something you'll have to think about. Depending on their attachment to friends in the church, they may have a much harder time adjusting than you expected.

My parents tell of a time years ago when they felt called to leave one church and start attending another one in the area. Though most of us were too young to care, my oldest brother, Walter, was not at all happy about the decision. At the age of six he had already built an emotional tie to the church and his friends in Sunday school.

My mother realized that he might take the news pretty hard, so she took him aside to explain their reasons for leaving. Hard as she tried, though, he couldn't comprehend why they were leaving.

Eventually he got over it. Within a few months he had found new friends in the new church, and no resentment remained. But it was not an easy transition.

Fortunately for Mom and Dad, we were all fairly young at the time. But some of my friends who have left their churches are parents of teenagers, and their transitions were much more painful and long-lasting. A rule of thumb seems to be the older the child, the more difficult the change.

There is no foolproof method to make sure your children have a smooth transition to a different church. But your children should have been involved in every step of the reevaluation process. The six-step plan for survival is designed to involve the entire family. This is important, because kids need to feel ownership in the decision whatever it happens to be—especially since it directly affects them. They need to feel that God is guiding the entire family, not just Mom and Dad. My guess is that when they understand that, the transition will inevitably be easier for them.

Be as sensitive as possible to their feelings. The change will not be easy on you, and it will be even harder on them. Give your kids the freedom to be angry, if that's how they feel. Let them go through stages of grief and sadness. It may even make sense to let them visit their old church from time to time, if that proves to make things easier for them.

But *don't* let them disrupt the family and overthrow the decision to leave. Be loving but firm, patient but unwavering. The decision needs to stand. And families should always stand together.

Finding a New Church Home

It goes without saying that if you've felt a call to leave your church home, you will soon be in search of another congregation to attend. And though a plan for finding a new church home is beyond the scope of this book, it makes sense to discuss a few do's and don'ts of the procedure.

In *Finding a Church You Can Call Home* George Barna offers principles to help people find the church that is right for them. If you're in need of a church—or just interested in a good read—I highly recommend this fine book. Having conducted extensive surveys, he put together a list of the most-often-cited criteria people use for evaluating a church. He does not set up

the items in any particular order of importance, but offers it to
help readers sort out their own wants and needs in a church
home:

1. The spiritual beliefs of the church.
2. The life-styles of the church members.
3. The denominational affiliation of the church.
4. The ability to make meaningful relationships with people
in the church.
5. The potential for using your skills and talents to serve
others, or to experience personal fulfillment.
6. The ability to have a significant worship experience.
7. The size of the congregation.
8. The depth of vision and quality of leadership evident within
the church.
9. The special programs the church operates (e.g., Sunday
school, small group Bible studies, missions projects, etc.).
10. The location of the church and its members in relation to
your home.
11. The facilities and equipment owned by the church.[2]

Though you may have other criteria to add to the list, this is a
good place to start. Barna suggests prioritizing your criteria
beginning with the most important thing you need in a church
and ending with the least important.

You are not going to find a perfect church, because such a
church doesn't exist. But you can find one that has the qualities
you most want and need. Your goal is to determine those qualities and then begin looking.

I'll give you one other bit of advice from the pages of a good
book by another of my favorite authors—Tony Campolo. If I
were looking for a new church home, I would clip this excerpt
and tape it to my bedroom mirror. In fact, I may do that anyway,
just to keep my church on its toes!

Be careful that the particular congregation of the church you join is alive in Christ, has a nurturing fellowship, and has a deep sense of responsibility toward each of its members. Look for a community of believers that will enable you to feel loved and looked after. Make sure that the church you join is made up of real people who can be honest with one another and who are not ashamed to confess their sins one to another. Be certain that it has a membership that is deeply involved in a collective prayer life and that its people know how to worship in dynamic ways that create an awareness of the Holy Spirit.

I know that what I am calling for is a tall order. But if the ongoing work of salvation is to be realized and enjoyed, then being connected to a church that is alive in the Holy Spirit is essential.

Some churches are dead. You can feel the deadness when you walk into their morning worship services. Do not waste your time on dead churches. You need to wear the helmet of salvation, and only a vital church can offer one to you.[3]

Taking the Leap

Shopping for a new church home does not rank among my favorite things to do. You may enjoy the excursion, but I dread it. I'm into stability. Consistency. Like the old horses that can't wait to get back to the barn where everything's comfortable.

Ruthie and I have very recently been called to use our gifts in a different church. Since the conflicts our former church had been through were in the past, the transition was not as hard as it could have been. There were no hard feelings on anyone's part. Still, making the change was not easy.

Though we've settled into our new church and ministry, we feel sadness over leaving good friends behind. But God called us to leave, and we're committed to following him.

Staying in our previous church during its time of turmoil proved to be a valuable and rewarding experience for us. We saw the wounds heal and were able to help the church move forward toward a new vision. It was difficult to later find ourselves being called to move on, but God's hand was clearly in the decision, and he has been with us every step of the way.

Perhaps you feel that God is telling you to move on, but you're having trouble taking that first step of faith. You want to obey, to be in God's will, to heed the still small voice in your soul, but the open door looks much too dark and frightening. Maybe you've found yourself clinging to the door jamb with all your might, hoping the voice would stop calling and the door would close shut.

If so, I encourage you to trust God. Trust him with your fears, your needs, your reservations. Trust him to calm your spirit and give you strength. And trust him to lead you to the church and the ministry he has already picked out for you.

The Christian life is an adventure like no other you will ever find. Nothing can compare to the excitement of following God on this marvelous journey, of being a part of a plan so big, so thrilling and so right for us. In the life of a vibrant Christian there need never be a dull moment.

I love the way Lee Strobel describes what it was like when he first gave his life to Christ and trusted God with his future:

Thrills that fulfill are those thrills that come when you truly submit your life to God and you pray a dangerous prayer like, "Here I am, Lord, wholly available to You."

These are the thrills you feel when God uses you to have an impact on other human beings that will last for eternity.

They're the thrills that come when God gives you a role to play in the biggest adventure of all time—the building of His kingdom.

It's the thrill that comes as you feel the glow of God's approval when you've been obedient to Him and when you've extended His love to people in need.

It's the thrill that comes when you pour yourself into the lives of others, and you witness how God begins to work in them, to transform them, cleanse them, relieve their guilt, and give their lives meaning and security. You're part of that!

It's the thrill you feel when you go out in faith onto a limb and say, "Lord, I'm going out further than I've ever gone before, and I'm scared. My heart's pounding and my palms are sweaty, but I know You'll protect me, so here I go."[4] Leaving your church body and trusting God to lead you to your new home is a frightening undertaking. But if God is leading, if he is in control, you have nothing to fear. And you have everything to gain.

Take a chance. Take that great leap of faith. Following God is the greatest, most rewarding roller-coaster ride on earth. Life doesn't get any better!

12

STEP SIX: SETTLE IN AND SETTLE DOWN!

I tease a friend of mine for being unable to find a church that he can connect with. I call him a "professional church-hopper." He changes churches every few years, always looking for something better—better friends, better leaders, better preaching, better music, a better prayer life . . . And always when he finds a new church he's convinced that *this* is finally the perfect church for him. A few months or years later he wonders how the church could have changed so much since he joined it, and once again he's shopping around.

My friend knows I love him. But I still think he needs to settle down and find a church that he can call home. Some place that isn't perfect in every way, but where he can feel comfortable and useful. Some place that is vibrant and growing and working hard at furthering God's kingdom on earth in spite of its inevitable flaws and shortcomings.

Too many of us expect more out of our church than we expect from ourselves. We're quick to overlook our own frailties and imperfections, but when it comes to church we expect perfection—100 percent health on every count. "There's no room for error in the household of God!"

And so when our church drops the ball on an issue or two, we're out the door, once again looking for a flawless church.

George Barna has some good arguments against this kind of thinking:

It is wrong to flit from church to church every time something goes contrary to your own personal whims or desires. The church is our spiritual family, and just as divorce is not to be held as a trump card in our marital relations, neither is dumping one church for another an act that we should take lightly, or do with any regularity.

As you commit yourself to a church, you will find many advantages in sticking with that church for the long haul. By accepting the congregation as your church home, you will have an easier time making deep and lasting friendships. You will have a greater range and number of opportunities to be involved in activities and decision-making at the church. Longevity within the church may enhance your own feeling of roots and stability and help reduce your anxiety level. Perhaps more importantly, you will also be setting an example of commitment for new Christians and for youth.[1]

Until this point you've been putting your churches through a rigorous test, but now it's time to turn the spotlight on yourself for a while. Whenever we are unhappy with a church situation we need to examine our own motives and attitudes, to see if we're not expecting more than any church is able to offer. To see if our needs and desires are realistic and reachable. And to see if perhaps the problem doesn't lie with our church but with us.

Self-examination is an important element in authentic, growing faith. David prayed that God would continually keep his heart and motives right:

Search me, O God, and know my heart;
    test me and know my anxious thoughts.
See if there is any offensive way in me,
    and lead me in the way everlasting. (Psalm 139:23-24)

Sincere disciples of Christ are willing to reevaluate their desires and attitudes and conduct on a regular basis, to peek into the closet of the heart to see if any unaddressed sin lingers hidden in the dark.

For the final step in the six-step plan for survival, let's stop and ask some important, soul-searching questions. The key to much of the conflict you've felt in the church may very well be found somewhere in the next few pages.

1. How Is My Relationship with God?

This is what's known in journalism circles as a "firehose question." It's when you hit someone straight on with all you've got—getting right to the core of things.

If our relationship with God is not what it should be, nothing else in our lives will seem right either—including our attitudes and feelings about our church.

I was once talking with a woman about the strife her church was feeling. "The leaders say that our problems stem from the fact that we're not evangelizing enough," she said. "They're starting to stress outreach and think that will solve the problems. But I think the problem is that we haven't fallen in love with the Lord. Before we evangelize the community, we need to evangelize ourselves!"

What an insightful comment. If we want to help change the world with the message of Christ, shouldn't we first see that our own lives have been changed by that message?

How is your prayer life? Do you spend time with the Lord every

day, praying for guidance and strength? Bill Hybels defines
prayer as "the key to unlocking God's prevailing power in your
life."[2] The power to change our lives, our church, our conflicts
is already in place—if only we are willing to tap into it.

Do you spend time in private devotion? Do you have a regular time
of reading and meditating on God's Word? Have you fallen in
love with the Scriptures? The psalmist proclaimed,

I seek you with all my heart;
> do not let me stray from your commands.
I have hidden your word in my heart
> that I might not sin against you. (Psalm 119:10-11)

Can you make that same claim?

Is your time of worship meaningful and authentic? When you praise
God in the assembly, are your words sincere? Do you praise him
throughout the day—at home, in the car, during a walk through
the park? Psalm 150 paints a beautiful picture of what it means
to praise God with all our hearts:

Praise the LORD.
Praise God in his sanctuary;
> praise him in his mighty heavens.
Praise him for his acts of power;
> praise him for his surpassing greatness.
Praise him with the sounding of the trumpet,
> praise him with the harp and lyre,
praise him with tambourine and dancing,
> praise him with the strings and flute,
praise him with the clash of cymbals,
> praise him with resounding cymbals.
Let everything that has breath praise the LORD.
Praise the LORD.

2. Do I Encourage Others?

I once taught a thirteen-week course in a church we were

attending. I was confident of my material, but the class was made up of many of the older members of the church and had always been taught by a pastor or elder. At thirty-five, I was the youngest person to ever teach in the class, and I had to work overtime at gaining the members' respect and trust.

One member, Jeanine, a kind, goodhearted woman, sensed my struggles to win the class over and took it upon herself to encourage me every chance she had. After each class she made her way to the front to tell me how much she appreciated what I had said. She often reminded me of a passage in Scripture that backed up my views—sometimes one that I hadn't even known about. She went out of her way to be an encouragement to me. I looked forward to seeing her smiling face each week.

More than any person I know, Jeanine seems unaffected by conflict in the church. She simply doesn't let it bother her. Through it all she keeps on smiling, keeps on encouraging. What an example she has been to me and others.

That's what the writer of Hebrews had in mind when he told us to "spur one another one toward love and good deeds" (10:24). Nothing will create a greater sense of love and unity among God's people than a basic feeling of optimism and encouragement. We all need it. And we all need to give it.

Karl Menninger describes people as having either a "Yes face" or a "No face." In his book *The Vital Balance* he tells of a time when Thomas Jefferson was traveling on horseback through the countryside with a group of companions. They came to a river and found that the bridge had been washed away by a recent rain. The only way across was to have their horses swim through the treacherous currents. Each rider took his life into his hands as they crossed. There was a good chance that some of them would not survive.

A traveler who was not part of the group was watching from a distance. Having seen several riders brave the currents, he walked up to the president and asked if he could ride across with him. Jefferson quickly agreed, and they took off across the water.

When they arrived safely on the other side, the man slid off the saddle and onto the ground. One of the men from the president's group asked him, "Tell me, why did you select the president to ask this favor of?"

Surprised, the man admitted that he hadn't known it was the president who had helped him across. "All I know," he said, "is that on some of your faces was written the answer 'No,' and on some of them was the answer 'Yes.' His was a 'Yes' face."[3]

Is yours a "Yes" face or a "No" face? Are you an encourager or a discourager?

3. Do I Use My Spiritual Gifts?

"Unless you become involved in the activities of your church," says Barna, "you will never truly feel satisfied with that church." He continues:

> This may seem a bit strong and may even conflict with your interest in attending a church. However, most people who attend church and feel that the church is inspiring, fulfilling and adding something special to their lives, are the people who do more than simply attend services on Sunday mornings. They are characterized by involvement in the practical ministry activities of the church. . . .
>
> It seems, then, that the old adage is true: You only get out of a church as much as you put into it.[4]

The sum total of a church is simply the people who make it up. When people come together, pooling their talents and resources for the good of the whole, the result is a church body that is alive and growing. And as Paul wrote, just as our physical body has many parts and members, so does a church body:

> Just as each of us has one body with many members, and these members do not all have the same function, so in Christ we

who are many form one body, and each member belongs to all the others. We have different gifts, according to the grace given us. If a man's gift is prophesying, let him use it in proportion to his faith. If it is serving, let him serve; if it is teaching, let him teach; if it is encouraging, let him encourage; if it is contributing to the needs of others, let him give generously; if it is leadership, let him govern diligently; if it is showing mercy, let him do it cheerfully. (Romans 12:4-8)

There is nothing like watching a group of believers functioning as one body, each person doing his or her part to help the church move toward a common goal to honor Christ.

Do you know your spiritual gifts? Are you using those gifts for the good of the church?

4. Do I Pray for My Church and Its Leaders?

Some friends of mine recently joined a very fast-growing, Bible-centered church. They've had many good things to say about the church, but the thing that impresses them most is the emphasis on prayer—specifically, prayer for the church body and leadership. One of the church's core ministries is a group that gathers on a weekly basis to pray for the congregation. And when my friends filled out a card pledging membership, they were encouraged to also sign a statement promising to spend one day per week praying for the church and its many programs and ministries.

More churches should encourage prayer among their members. Nothing will bring a body closer together than collective prayer.

Several things happen when we decide to pray for our church regularly and systematically.

☐ *We take the focus off ourselves and place it on Christ.* Much of the conflict in churches can be traced back to a "navel-gazing" mentality. Navel-gazing breeds selfishness and immaturity, while prayer teaches us to love God and each other.

☐ *Prayer brings people together for a unified purpose.* Praying for our church helps us keep the church's purpose and vision in mind. When we unite to pray for the church, the leaders, the pastors, the ministries and each other, we are reminding God and ourselves that we are a family—that we are committed not to ourselves but to the good of the group.

☐ *Prayer acknowledges that it is God who has the answers, not us.* Like the mother reminding her young daughter before the school prom, "Don't forget to dance with the one who brung ya!" we need to remember that it is Christ's church we are a part of, not ours. It is he who brought us together. It is God and God alone who has the answers to our many questions and the cure for the church's many ailments. Prayer reminds us that God is in control. We are serving him.

☐ *Things happen when we pray.* Powerful things happen when Christians come together to pray. Dragons are slain daily through the simple prayers of meek and gentle warriors. There is no church conflict that God cannot—and will not—help us overcome if we simply humble ourselves and ask him.

5. Am I Involved in Relationship Building?

In *The Lonely Pew* Doug Fagerstrom and James Carlson talk of Christians' need to build meaningful relationships with one another in the church:

> A lot of lonely people live in our present culture and sit in our churches. We all need friends and family. God created us as social beings, an imperative for normal living by his design and will. However, finding friends and family can become an exhausting and discouraging experience for many, especially those whose middle name is introvert.[5]

Most churches are aware of this need and have set up a number of relationship-building programs and ministries. The problem comes when members don't take advantage of these programs.

I know people who are very involved in church work. They take it upon themselves to do many needed tasks and chores. But still they seem unhappy and unfulfilled. So they volunteer for even more projects, hoping that will fill the void. The problem is, these people aren't building relationships. They are too busy keeping the church running to find time for small groups, men's and women's ministries, prayer groups, retreats, potlucks and the like.

We all need to be connected with others. And if our church has implemented programs to fill that need and we haven't taken advantage of them, we have no one to blame but ourselves.

Though Ruthie and I have several close friends at our present church, there are times when we find ourselves feeling lonely and isolated. Invariably, when we discuss these feelings with each other we realize that it has been a good while since we instigated a get-together. We remedy the situation by having friends over for dinner or scheduling a night out with a few people.

We've found that unless we take an active role in cultivating and maintaining friendships, we usually find ourselves feeling left out and alone. And unhappy.

6. Do I Support My Church Financially?

Most of us are willing to give to causes we believe in. Time and again church leaders have found that when members feel strongly about a need—when they develop ownership in a drive to raise funds—they will do whatever it takes to meet that need.

Not long ago California was hit very hard by a series of earthquakes. Many people lost their homes and possessions. Our church elders announced that we would be taking up a special collection for the victims of this earthquake, and it was inspiring how freely and generously people gave.

Charles Stanley tells of a time when his congregation dug

deeper than they ever thought they could to buy some property for expansion to their facility. A block and a half of property adjacent to their building became available for $2,850,000. Over a twelve-month period the church members raised $1,350,000 toward the purchase, but they were still short $1,500,000. Stanley was convinced that God wanted them to buy the land, but he was equally convinced that they should not borrow the money (this occurred in 1981, when interest rates were at 21 percent).

The deadline to purchase the land was just two days away, and he didn't know how they could possibly raise the remaining money in time. "It looked impossible," he wrote, "especially in light of how much the people had already given."

During his prayers that Saturday night, God put a conviction in his heart not to give up. "Trust me!" he felt God telling him.

When I stepped into the pulpit on the following Sunday with the deadline 24 hours away, we still needed an additional $1,500,000. As I looked out across the sea of faces, it all seemed so impossible. But I knew what I had to do. God and I had settled that the day before. . . .

As I shared this challenge with the people, I made it clear that we wouldn't borrow any money. "We must burn every bridge and cut off every avenue of escape. Our faith must be in Him and Him alone," I said. . . .

By that Sunday evening they gave an additional $1 million. Thirty minutes before the deadline we had our $2,850,000.[6]

Jesus said, "Where your treasure is, there your heart will be also" (Matthew 6:21). If we love and believe in our church—if our heart is there—we will gladly and willingly give to further the work it is doing.

7. Am I an Angel of Peace or an Agent of Discord?

Some people are simply born for conflict. They love to argue.

We all know people who will go out of their way to provoke a good argument.

Years ago I knew a man who was the consummate quarreler. He and I didn't see eye to eye on anything. Regardless of the topic, we always seemed to be on different wavelengths. I would make a statement, and immediately he would refute it. It was hard for me to be around him—our constant disagreements wore on my nerves and conscience. So I became determined to do something about it—to find at least one thing we agreed on.

One day during a church business meeting, the discussion turned to a future expansion to the building. My friend made a comment that I felt was right on target. He suggested some ways to cut costs by trimming some of the frills out of the architect's plans. "This is God's money we are spending," he began, "and we should be careful that we don't waste it."

Later I took him aside. "I really appreciated your words," I told him. "I think we need to be better stewards of God's money and make sure we're not being wasteful."

Without hesitation he turned to me and said, "Well, there's also a lot to be said for pushing ourselves and dreaming a little. When Mary poured the bottle of perfume over Jesus' feet, the disciples called it a waste of money, and Jesus told them off for it. Maybe we shouldn't be so quick to call these extras wasteful."

I couldn't believe it! Here I was merely reiterating his earlier words, and still he argued with me. After that I no longer took our disagreements personally. I simply considered the source. He loved to argue, and he assumed that everyone else did as well.

There are people like that in every church. In fact, some people wouldn't feel at home if they couldn't find something or someone to complain about every Sunday.

The problem with that kind of personality (or habit) is that it can easily cause dissension in the church. People who enjoy arguing need to find a better place and a better way to vent that desire. Arguing for the sake of argument is out of place in the body of Christ. The writer of Proverbs says, "He who loves a quarrel loves sin" (17:19).

Are you a messenger of peace or an agent of discord? Do you work at getting along or spend your time just looking for a good argument?

Settle In and Settle Down

Whether you've decided to stay with your present church or look for another church home, it's important now to look forward—to *move* forward. There's no reason to allow the past to repeat itself.

All people are fallen. As long as churches are made up of people there will be disagreements and conflicts. But if you've been a big part of the problem in your church, it's time to repent and change. Forgive others for their flaws, then forgive yourself. And most important, pledge that with God's help you will work at changing your attitudes and actions.

Commit yourself to your church—heart and soul. Then settle in and settle down.

I end this chapter—and this section of the book—with some words from Paul encouraging all of us simply to be kind to each other. Even when we disagree.

Do not let any unwholesome talk come out of your mouths, but only what is helpful for building others up according to their needs, that it may benefit those who listen. And do not grieve the Holy Spirit of God, with whom you were sealed for the day of redemption. Get rid of all bitterness, rage and anger, brawling and slander, along with every form of malice. Be kind and compassionate to one another, forgiving each other, just as in Christ God forgave you. (Ephesians 4:29-32)

PART III

IN DEFENSE
OF A LITTLE
UNITY

13

EXPOSING THE "PEACE-BUSTERS"

*P*oor Anna wasn't looking for trouble. All she wanted was to come to church and worship with her fellow believers. And the most sacred part of the service to her was Communion. But her church was so disorganized that it couldn't seem to get Communion right.

It all started early one Sunday morning when Bob, the new pastor, received a call from the people in charge of preparing for the service. "We forgot to get the grape juice for this morning's Communion and the stores are all closed," they told him. "We were wondering if you might have some at your house."

He didn't. But he did have a bottle of juice that was made from "fruit of the vine." It was much tarter than they were used to, but they decided it would have to do.

When Anna took her cup, she was not happy. She was convinced that it was wine, and everyone knew she had never taken a drink of anything made with alcohol. Never. "I promise it has not fermented," Bob assured her. "It just tastes that way." Anna wasn't totally convinced, but she took the pastor's word and drank it.

Two weeks later Bob's phone rang again. "We tried all day yesterday to find some grape juice, but everyone was out of it. Do you happen to have some more of the juice you brought last time?"

He didn't. He did have a bottle of another kind of juice. "But this one is rather sweet," he told them. They had no choice but to use it.

Again, Anna was not happy. "This just doesn't taste at all like fruit of the vine," she told them. "It tastes more like Kool-Aid." Bob assured her that it wasn't, and once more she took his word for it.

Three weeks later, another phone call. "We didn't forget the grape juice," the committee told him. "But we couldn't find our regular brand. The one we got is clear instead of burgundy. Do you think it will matter?" Bob wasn't sure, but it was too late to try to find an alternative.

This time Anna nearly hit the ceiling. "This looks like water!" she exclaimed. "Or some kind of white wine."

It took Bob a while to settle her down and explain that grapes are indeed different colors, but each kind is still a "fruit of the vine." She acquiesced but still wondered if someone wasn't up to something.

Bob considered not even answering the phone when it rang again early the next Sunday morning. But he knew he had to.

"Bob, we really hate to keep doing this to you, but we've got another problem. We got the grape juice, but we couldn't find any unleavened bread. What do you think we should do?"

Since there were no stores open for miles around, the only solution he could think of was to call some area churches and see if they could help. A few calls were made, and soon a kind priest from a Catholic church gladly offered to loan them some. Bob thanked him and promptly directed the committee members to pick up the bread.

He thought the matter had been solved until he saw Anna's mouth drop wide open as she took the Communion tray. Bob made his way over to where she was sitting to see what was the matter, and there in the tray was a handful of small round wafers, each with a little cross on the front and some Latin writing across the top.

He had hoped the committee would have the sense to break them up before putting them into the tray.

That day after services Anna announced that she was putting herself in charge of getting supplies for Communion. The committee surrendered to her wishes. And the church never had a problem with it again.

"Peace-Busters" on the Loose!

Most of us don't go looking for conflict in the church, but it happens just the same. Sometimes the problems are unintentional and rather harmless—like the ones that poor Anna went through—and other times they are mean-spirited and brutal.

Some conflicts are caused by simple miscommunication. Someone says one thing and others hear something else.

Some conflicts are caused by selfishness. Two people find themselves at odds over an issue, and neither one is willing to concede his wants and preferences.

Some conflicts are caused by doctrinal differences. The same passage of Scripture can mean one thing to one person and something entirely different to another.

Some conflicts are caused by blatant sin. A pastor divorces his wife and takes up with the church secretary, and the church polarizes into camps of support and nonsupport.

But regardless of the cause, conflict can be devastating. It can often lead to long-term resentment within a church body.

And it can cause otherwise happy and peaceful churches to become battlegrounds of strife and dissension.

Though a certain amount of conflict in the church is inevitable, one key to maintaining peace is to keep friction to a minimum and then effectively manage the problems that do arise.

Conflict management will be addressed in the next chapter. But for now let's take a closer look at some of the more common "peace-busters" in today's churches.

The Me Factor

James keenly summed up the most common cause of conflict within the body of Christ in his letter to the churches:

> What causes fights and quarrels among you? Don't they come from your desires that battle within you? You want something but don't get it. You kill and covet, but you cannot have what you want. You quarrel and fight. You do not have, because you do not ask God. When you ask, you do not receive, because you ask with wrong motives, that you may spend what you get on your pleasures. (James 4:1-3)

Simply put, most fights in churches can be traced back to self-centeredness—to wanting our own way regardless of the feelings and needs of others.

The same is true in my household. There are few fights between my kids that can't be traced to the "me factor." "That belongs to me!" "I was playing with that first!" "She won't play what I want to play!" Each child wants his or her own way, and when they don't get it, they fight and argue.

We adults behave like children in this way all too often, don't we? When it comes to church we all want our own way. We want the songs and song leaders we like, the times to fit our schedules, the money spent the way we would spend it and the sermons to be relevant to our lifestyles.

Woe to the deacon who runs fifteen minutes long in her presentation from the pulpit about a new ministry idea. By the time we get to our favorite restaurant there's a twenty-minute wait. And don't think somebody isn't going to hear about it!

The me factor has caused more fights, more conflict, more resignations, more pastor firings and more church splits than all the other peace-busters put together.

When all the dust settled after the split at our church and we were able to look back and analyze the causes, it was easy to see that the me factor was the true culprit behind most of the conflicts.

Majoring in the Minors

Pettiness is the archenemy of unity. When churches and people get caught up in narrow-minded, insignificant issues, love and harmony fly out the window. When we worry more about whether someone is going to raise their hands during worship or clap at an inappropriate time or read a Scripture wearing blue jeans than we do about praising God or evangelizing our community, there is something wrong with our lives and our priorities. Satan wins many a battle with this simple, all-too-common tool—convincing God's people to major in the minors.

Mike Yaconelli, editor of *The Door,* has had some cutting words to say about pettiness in the church.

Petty people are ugly people. They are people who have lost their vision. They are people who have turned their eyes away from what matters and focused, instead, on what doesn't matter. The result is that the rest of us are immobilized by their obsession with the insignificant. It is time to rid the church of pettiness. It is time the church refused to be victimized by petty people. It is time the church stopped ignoring pettiness. It is time the church quit pretending that pettiness doesn't matter.

. . . Pettiness has become a serious disease in the Church of Jesus Christ—a disease which continues to result in terminal cases of discord, disruption, and destruction. Petty people are dangerous people because they appear to be only a nuisance instead of what they really are—a health hazard.[1]

Pettiness is sitting with your arms crossed and your jaws tightened in protest when you don't like the songs or the pitch at which they're sung.

Pettiness is firing off a heated letter to church leaders when a teenager's haircut doesn't meet with your approval or a young father shows up at church in tennis shorts because he didn't have time to change.

Pettiness is boycotting a special baby-dedication service because your kids are already grown and gone—and because those kinds of services are not "decent and orderly" in your way of thinking.

Pettiness is majoring in the minors. And God's people should be above it.

Legalism

Daniel Taylor defines legalism as "the manufacturing and manipulation of rules for the purpose of illegitimate control." He goes on: "Legalism clings to law at the expense of grace, to the letter in place of the spirit."[2]

Legalism is a peace-buster that has hurt more people, crippled more projects, killed more enthusiasm than any of us care to count. It's when we spend more time listing things we "can't" do than dreaming about the things we can.

In a nutshell, legalism is trying to get to heaven on your own deeds—by holding to the letter of the law and ignoring the spirit of it. Legalism nullifies God's grace.

Legalism was at the heart of Paul's concerns when he wrote to the churches of Galatia:

You foolish Galatians! Who has bewitched you? Before your very eyes Jesus Christ was clearly portrayed as crucified. I would like to learn just one thing from you: Did you receive the Spirit by observing the law, or by believing what you heard? Are you so foolish? After beginning with the Spirit, are you now trying to attain your goal by human effort? Have you suffered so much for nothing—if it really was for nothing? Does God give you his Spirit and work miracles among you because you observe the law, or because you believe what you heard? (Galatians 3:1-5)

Just today I heard the story of a missionary who died of cancer several years ago. He had devoted his entire life to preaching the Word of God to people around the world. He raised a wonderful Christian family and served as spiritual father to many other people. Yet on his deathbed he lay with tears in his eyes, pouring out his fears to a fellow minister: "I just hope I've done enough for the Lord. I'm so afraid he won't accept me!"

What heavy and unnecessary burdens we carry when we come under the oppression of legalism.

Chuck Swindoll has this to say about legalism:

In so many words, legalism says, "I do this or I don't do that, and therefore I am pleasing God." Or "If only I could do this or not do that I would be pleasing to God." Or perhaps, "These things that I'm doing or not doing are the things I perform to win God's favor." They aren't spelled out in Scripture, you understand. They've been passed down or they have been dictated to the legalist and have become an obsession to him or her. Legalism is rigid, grim, exacting, and lawlike in nature. Pride, which is at the heart of legalism, works in sync with other motivating factors. Like guilt. And fear. And shame. It leads to an emphasis on what should not be, and what one should not do. It flourishes in a drab context of negativism.[3]

When churches fall prey to legalism, they lose their soul—their heart. They've missed the entire point of Calvary, choosing instead to rely on their own abilities and accomplishments. The legalist is a master at taking Scripture out of context to make a point. Proof-texts fly in any argument. And legalists are seldom right in their interpretations, because their point of view is biased and skewed.

What a sad way to live. And what a breeding ground for conflict it creates!

Gossip

When I think of gossip, I think of a particular old country church deep in the South. Every church has at least one eccentric couple, and this church's prime candidates were Bill and Verna.

Bill was up in age—somewhere around eighty—and Verna was not far behind. When they moved into the neighborhood, no one knew quite what to think of them. They were sweet, but different.

For instance, every Sunday morning they would walk down the center aisle of the church and split company about halfway down. Bill sat on the left side of the sanctuary, Verna sat on the right. Always. Even on their first Sunday there. As far as I know, no one ever asked them why, and they never bothered to explain. "That's just Bill and Verna's way," people figured.

One day a rumor started floating around the church. "All Verna ever feeds Bill is oatmeal," someone said. "Three meals a day, seven days a week! It's all she lets him eat."

It was a strange rumor, and no one knew quite what to do with it. But one of the ladies was convinced it was true. "In fact, I think she's trying to kill him," she added. "A person can't live on just oatmeal. She knows that. What else can it be?"

The couple obviously weren't very close, they decided. They never sat together in church, and not one person could remember hearing them even speak to each other. "Yep, that must be it," they concluded. "Verna's trying to kill her husband. And when he dies, she'll plead ignorance and likely get away with it."

Someone had to stop her. "Let's get the minister," someone suggested. "He'll know what to do." And so they did.

It took several weeks before the minister was convinced that he needed to get involved. And by the time he did, the rumor was running at full throttle. It got to the point where a hush descended every time Bill and Verna walked into the sanctuary. The middle aisle parted like the Red Sea as they walked toward their seats each week. Whether the rumor was true or not, the pastor knew he needed to step in and clear the air.

With his hat in his hand, he went to visit the elderly couple. And like most rumors, this one proved to be unfounded.

"Now, why on earth would I want to kill Bill?" Verna inquired as the pastor stood red-faced, staring down at the floor. "I never heard such a silly thing in all my life."

"Well, they say you only feed him oatmeal . . ." he ventured.

"You think I'd expect him to live on nothing but oatmeal?" she came back indignantly. "Yes, he eats a lot of oatmeal. Most of the time that's all the old goat'll eat. He hasn't got a tooth in his head. What am I supposed to do, let him gnaw on a steak every night? He likes oatmeal, and that's what he wants. So I give it to him. As if it's anybody's business anyway!"

Needless to say, the pastor watched where he stuck his nose from then on. And I'll bet he's preached more than a few sermons on the evils of gossip.

Gossip is a very real problem—in offices, in neighborhoods and in the church. All of us have been victims of untrue rumors at one time or another. Such rumors can hurt people badly.

I once knew a kind, godly woman who attended a conservative, nondenominational church. She was an example of Christian love, compassion and servanthood to all who knew her. One day someone started a rumor that she had advocated tongue-speaking in a class she was teaching. Within weeks the rumor gained momentum, and the gossip mill soon had it that she was not only advocating it but doing it—and closing the doors of her classroom to help others speak in tongues as well. People pictured this kind woman holding a Pentecostal revival, behind closed doors, right under the noses of the elders.

It was the most ridiculous rumor any of us had ever heard. The woman's friends dismissed it immediately. But the harm had already been done. Years later, long after the gossip had been proven unfounded, she still felt the effects. Her husband was even passed over as a candidate for elder because of the presumed harm done to the family's reputation.

Nothing good ever comes out of gossip. And many a church conflict has been caused by this all-too-common sin of the tongue.

Miscommunication

No one knows more about miscommunication than the Reverend A. J. Jones of Pretoria, South Africa. Let me tell you his story.

It started when he ran a classified ad in the local newspaper. The first day the ad appeared, it read:

> The Rev. A. J. Jones has a color TV set for sale. Telephone 555-1313 after 7 p.m. and ask for Mrs. Donnelley who lives with him, cheap.

He wasn't happy, and he called to let the folks at the paper know. So the next day they tried to undo their mistake. The new ad read:

> We regret any embarrassment caused to Rev. Jones by a typographical error in yesterday's edition. It should have read, "The Rev. A. J. Jones has color TV set for sale, cheap. Telephone 555-1313 and ask for Mrs. Donnelley who lives with him after 7 p.m."

Another call was made, and again they tried to fix the confusion.

The Rev. A. J. Jones informs us he has received several annoying telephone calls because of an incorrect advertisement in yesterday's paper. It should have read, "The Rev. A. J. Jones has color TV set for sale. Cheap. Telephone after 7 p.m. 555-1313 and ask for Mrs. Donnelley who loves with him."
One day later . . .
Please take note that I, the Rev. Jones, have no TV set for sale. I have smashed it. I have not been carrying on with Mrs. Donnelley. She was until yesterday my housekeeper.
You would have thought that would end the ordeal, but if you watched closely, you saw another ad a few days later that read:
WANTED: a housekeeper. Telephone the Rev. A. J. Jones, 555-1313. Usual housekeeping duties, good pay, love in.[4]
I assume he gave up trying.

Much conflict in churches can be traced to simple acts of miscommunication. Someone says one thing and someone else hears another. And because feelings are usually involved, the misunderstanding almost always gets blown out of proportion.

An older man in a church in the Midwest once heard of the leader's plans to use a quartet during the service to help members distinguish the different singing parts. He was convinced that the plan was to organize a choir—something this church had never had or wanted. He relayed to several other members what he thought was going to happen, and they too became disgruntled. Instead of taking their concerns to the leaders, they let the matter escalate until a group left and started another church. And all because of a simple act of miscommunication.

When Tradition Becomes Doctrine

Leith Anderson tells of a Lutheran church in a small Danish village that was steeped in tradition, some of which made no sense to anyone. As the people filed into the building each week, they walked down the center aisles to a plain white wall. Each worshiper would pause in front of the wall, turn, and genuflect with head bowed low and knees facing the wall. Then they would rise and work their way to their seats.

An observer was puzzled by this ritual and began asking both the clergy and the laity for an explanation. No one seemed to know. "We've always done it this way" was the only answer he received. He researched the matter further and found that hundreds of years earlier there had been an elaborate painting of the Virgin Mary on the wall that was now painted white. Before the Protestant Reformation the church had been used as a Roman Catholic cathedral, and when the Lutheran church took it over, the painting was washed out and painted over. But generations later the people were still bowing before the wall—a ritual that had originated with their Catholic predecessors. The tradition was meaningless to everyone, yet it persisted.[5]

Whenever I talk of the need to reevaluate traditions, I sense immediate disapproval. People usually miss the point. They think I love picking on traditions and consider all tradition useless. Nothing could be further from the truth.

Tradition is not a bad thing. In fact, most of what I do, what we all do, is rooted in tradition—from the clothes we wear to the hours we keep to the times we eat meals. I live in a traditional house in a traditional neighborhood, and I relish holiday traditions of all kinds.

The problem I have is with blind, purposeless, meaningless tradition—tradition with no point, no value and no significance, yet usually tied up with a great deal of emotion. Churches, by their very nature, have traditions—some of which are human-made, others of which are God-ordained. Traditions are an important part of the Christian faith. But when we lose sight of the point behind a tradition, when we give it a wrong priority, when the traditions we create become a part of our doctrine and just as sacred, we've burdened the gospel. *And* we've created a breeding ground for conflict in the church.

Traditions need to be kept in perspective and should be reevaluated and changed if the need arises.

A few simple questions about our traditions and rituals can help put them in the proper perspective:

☐ *Does the tradition originate from Christ or Scripture as an integral part of the Lord's church?* Many traditions are rooted in Scripture and have very clear meanings and purposes. Meeting together each week is a tradition with scriptural support. When we take Communion we are following through on Christ's direction for us to reenact his last meal with his apostles before his death. When we are baptized into his body, we are sharing in a wonderful tradition that has been practiced throughout the ages of the church. Jesus himself went into the water as an example for the rest of us to follow.

These are beautiful and important traditions of the church, and we shouldn't compromise on them. They are meaningful— both to Christ and to us. And they should remain an integral part of any church.

☐ *If the tradition is a human-made one, is it meaningful to the whole of the congregation?* One church we know of has a tradition of having the children come to the front of the auditorium and sing a few songs to the rest of the congregation before making their way to the children's Bible hour. They've only been doing it for a few years, yet it has already become a meaningful tradition to the church. It has served as a weekly reminder that the future of the church is with children—that the church is as much for them as it is for their parents. It is meaningful. It is fruitful. It is unifying. And it is a tradition worth hanging on to.

A church we once attended had an annual tradition of organizing a dedication for all the babies born during the year. Before the congregation, parents pledged to raise and nurture their children in the Lord, and the congregation pledged to stand behind them, doing all they could to help. Both groups then recited a short pledge, led by the pastor. It was a beautiful and unifying tradition. It had meaning and substance and purpose— the kind of tradition that churches need to keep.

□ *Does the tradition help or hinder efforts to reach the unchurched?* Most Christians have an honest desire to reach others for Christ. They want to bring their friends to church, to witness to them, to lead them into a relationship with Christ. But we often don't take the time think about what our traditions and services look like to outsiders. Our traditions often mean a lot to us but little or nothing to our unchurched friends.

Lee Strobel tells of a time he attended a church after seeing a large, impressive advertisement in the local newspaper. The ad was an honest effort to invite unchurched people to visit the church. Strobel was intrigued and went to check out the church for himself. Here's his report on the visit:

> The service started with someone's asking the congregation to sing along with a chorus for which no lyrics were provided. Regular attenders, of course, knew the words, but I felt awkward. Other hymns, accompanied by an organ, dated from 1869, 1871, and 1874, with such lyrics as, "Heav'nly portals loud with hosannas ring." . . .
>
> During the announcement time, a pastor directed newcomers to fill out a card "so we can put you on our mailing list." . . .
>
> The sermon, part of a series called "Issues in Christian Discipleship," quoted some experts, but they were all leaders of that denomination. . . . At the conclusion, he offered only two steps for people to take: Either turn over your life to Christ or commit yourself to deeper discipleship. . . .

Were these Christians doing anything inherently wrong? Of course not. I'm sure they were good, well-intentioned people who had a genuine desire to communicate the Gospel to unchurched people.

But were they really creating a service that would address the needs, concerns and longings of irreligious individuals? No, they weren't. By just doing church the way it always had been done, they had created an atmosphere where they felt comfortable but which would have chased away unchurched people.[6]

When what we do in church is unnecessarily alienating to those who desperately need to know God's love and goodness, it is time to reevaluate what we are doing. When traditions become ritualistic and comfortable to us but seem strange and meaningless to outsiders, maybe it is time for us to be a little less comfortable. Paul admonished us, "Be wise in the way you act toward outsiders; make the most of every opportunity" (Colossians 4:5).

Paul also said, "I have become all things to all men so that by all possible means I might save some" (1 Corinthians 9:22). That's the kind of attitude all of us need when it comes to our practices and traditions. To borrow one more line from Strobel: "The attitude, 'That's the way we've always done things' needs to become, 'What can we do better to meet more needs and reach more people with the Gospel?' "[7]

☐ *Is the tradition a unifying experience for the congregation, or is it boring, useless and repetitious (and divisive)?* A good friend recently told me of a couple he knew who attended a very small conservative church. The church met in a small space rented by the core group of five or six families. One Sunday the town got several feet of snow, and this husband and wife were the only members able to make it to the building. After waiting for a few minutes for the others, they decided they were on their own. So the wife sat in her regular seat as her husband stood at the podium. He said an opening prayer, read a Scripture, led them in three songs from the hymnal, preached a thirty-minute sermon, then led out in several choruses of "Just As I Am" as an invitation.

I thought my friend was joking, but he assured me that the

story was true—and that if I knew this couple and the church, I would understand how it could happen.

When we become so steeped in tradition that our services are lifeless and pointless, it's time to reevaluate them—and it's time to do some serious study of God's Word about what the meeting of the saints should be all about. It was never intended to be dominated by dull ritual. It was never intended that church become a series of meaningless, boring acts—a list of things we're supposed to do so we can say we've "done church" for the week and can feel free until the next Sunday morning.

When our services have become so encrusted in tradition that our tradition has *become* our religion, we have a problem. And pity the person who even suggests that we try to do things differently!

Congregations like this are a church fight just waiting to happen.

Unchecked Immorality

Many a church has felt the deep pain of immorality within the body, from pastors having affairs with church secretaries to deacons embezzling funds to couples within the church living together outside of marriage. Because we are human, we sin. And when sin is ignored, it tarnishes the church's effectiveness and reputation.

I once had a conversation with a single mother and was glad to find out that she attended church regularly. Until she started hanging out some of the church's dirty laundry. At least three of the female members of the church had illegitimate children by the pastor—including her. She insisted that she was still in love with him (as was one of the other women) and was staying in the church to try to lure him into marrying her.

When I showed surprise at the fact that he was still preaching there, she laughed and explained, "Oh, he almost got fired several times over it. He's slept with several women that I know of, even some married ones. But when he's caught, he cries and repents from the pulpit, and then we forgive him and go on. It's not like he's the only man in the church that's committed adultery."

Scripture is clear on how we need to view blatant, unrepented sin in the fellowship:

You must not associate with anyone who calls himself a brother but is sexually immoral or greedy, an idolater or a slanderer, a drunkard or a swindler. With such a man do not even eat. (1 Corinthians 5:11)

In the name of the Lord Jesus Christ, we command you, brothers, to keep away from every brother who is idle and does not live according to the teaching you received from us. (2 Thessalonians 3:6)

If anyone does not obey our instruction in this letter, take special note of him. Do not associate with him, in order that he may feel ashamed. (2 Thessalonians 3:14)

All of us need to be held accountable for our actions. We need "hedges" against temptation in our lives. And pastors are no exception to that rule. In fact, because of the isolated nature of their work, they probably need it more than we do.

I meet with a group of men each week so that we can discuss what is going on in our lives and the prayer needs we are feeling. We work at holding each other accountable as Christians, husbands and fathers. We confess sins and temptations and pray for strength to overcome them. Our weekly meeting been a wonderful tool for keeping us on track spiritually.

Unchecked sin only leads to greater sin and lesser sensitivity to any sin. And always, it causes strife in the church.

Power Politics

A church in Tennessee went through a devastating year when a pastor refused to leave after being fired by the church board. Just weeks earlier he had signed a one-year contract, and he refused to release the church from it. Though the board had hired another pastor to preach in his place, the first pastor kept his office and attended each week, sitting on the front row. All the while he collected his monthly check.

His appearance each week did nothing but add fuel to the resentment that was brewing. He kept in close touch with his supporters, who wanted to see him back in the pulpit and let that desire be known at every opportunity. They succeeded only in causing more strife and contention than ever.

The politics of power is another peace-buster that most churches are forced to deal with from time to time. To some, power means control over the physical functions of the church—the sanctuary, the education department, the board of deacons, the pulpit and the like. To others, it means controlling how the money is spent—which programs get funded, how much the preacher gets paid, how much is set aside for the future.

I served on the budget committee of our former church and have seen firsthand the conflicts that can arise over money concerns. Everyone has a different agenda. Everyone has a different idea about what is and isn't important. Our committee often felt great tension as it tried to distribute funds while remaining fair to everyone and partial to none.

Money means power. And power plays happen much too often within the church.

Doctrinal Differences

Leslie Flynn tells of a young man who joined a church but revealed a few months later that he didn't believe in the literal, bodily resurrection of Jesus. Over a period of time the leaders confronted him a number of times, trying to show him how he was wrong and why the issue was serious. But he persisted in denying this core element of the faith. Though it was a hard and painful thing to do, the leaders were eventually forced to disfellowship the young man and erase his name from the church membership list.[8]

Some beliefs are so clearly wrong that there should be little debate over how they should be handled. A denial of Jesus' resurrection is one of those.

But the rights and wrongs of most doctrinal differences within the church are not so clear. When people interpret the Bible to mean different things, we often have a doctrinal impasse.

☐ One person believes the Bible teaches a "once saved, always saved" message of salvation, another believes Christians can "fall away" from grace.

☐ One person is premillennial, another is postmillennial, still another is amillennial. (Donna Reeves, a good friend of mine, says she is *pan*millennial. "It'll all pan out in the end," she explains.)

☐ One person believes in the present-day gifts of the spirit (healings, tongues and so on), while another believes them to have passed away.

There is room for debate in these and many other areas of doctrine. But when we're convinced we are right on an issue, we are seldom accepting of another's viewpoint. And when those kinds of doctrinal differences occur within the same church body, you usually have quite a storm brewing.

Overcoming the "Peace-Busters"

There are other peace-busters we could list, to be sure. You've probably thought of a few of your own. In fact, you might have experienced a few of your own. The reasons Christians fight can be as different and varied as the Christians themselves. And as long as there are churches there will be church fights.

Peace-busters can bury a church so deep in conflict that it

never gets anything done. Leaders spend all their time putting out fires of discontent. Laypeople spend their time waiting and watching for the next feud. The church remains stagnant, never growing, and everyone wonders why.

There are times when we can't do much about that. We can't usually do much about what others do and say. And most of us are not in a position to lead the church toward peace and unity—to go to war against the peace-busters in our midst. But we can certainly keep our own attitudes in check. We can make sure that we are part of the solution instead of part of the problem.

The next chapter addresses that issue: how can you and I make sure we're not fueling the flames of unrest and division?

14

BECOMING A PEACE- BUSTER BUSTER

*A*uthor and lecturer Paul Faulkner tells of a time he was asked to counsel a couple having trouble in their marriage. They had built up years of resentment, he was told, and it would not be an easy marriage to fix. He agreed to see them.

On their first visit, Faulkner began by asking the couple what they thought might be the cause of their problems. Without hesitation the man rose to his feet, pointed his finger at his wife and said with a snarl, "That woman doesn't know the first thing about being married—that's the only thing wrong with this marriage!"

It didn't take Faulkner long to guess what the root of their problem might be. The more they talked, the more he saw just how difficult this man must be to live with. The husband spent the entire time listing his wife's faults, as she sat quietly in her chair.

"I know it takes two people to ruin a marriage," Faulkner says. "But this is one case where the husband was clearly the bigger rascal." The wife, he says, couldn't have been any kinder and more agreeable. Yet it never once occurred to that raging bull of a husband that he might be part of the problem.

People who cause conflict seldom see themselves as divisive or argumentative. They're often caught in the middle of controversy, but they don't usually suspect that they were responsible for starting it. Most of us aren't objective enough to see ourselves as we really are—or as others see us.

"Peace-busters" are usually the last to know that they have a problem.

If you and I are serious about becoming agents of peace in our churches, we need to make sure we're not adding to the conflict. We need to take a step back and look at ourselves from the outside—from the perspective of others. And we need to ask ourselves if we might need to change our ways of thinking, acting and talking.

Guarding the Tongue

Let's look now at some tough questions worth asking ourselves—questions that are designed to help separate the peace-busters from the peace-buster busters.

1. Do I keep my nose—and my opinion—where it belongs? Proverbs 26:17 says,

Like one who seizes a dog by the ears

is a passer-by who meddles in a quarrel not his own.

Some people can't resist jumping into the middle of a conflict whenever they find one. Police officers will tell you that one of the most frustrating parts of cleaning up the debris from a car accident is trying to keep passersby at a safe distance. People tend to be nosy and want to see what happened. Often they wonder if they can help. But all they are doing is getting in the way of those who need to be involved.

I've seen too many people in church eager to get involved in a conflict when it occurs. Sometimes they want to take sides, sometimes they want to help resolve it, other times they are simply being nosy.

Good advice for all of us is to keep our noses out of places and situations where they don't belong. If the conflict affects us somehow, if our name comes up or we see that we are about to be dragged into the struggle, then it is time to get involved. But if not—if we're just being nosy—we need to stay away and mind our own business.

2. Do I hold others—and myself—accountable for unfounded rumors and accusations? I had a friend once who refused to tolerate gossip. She had been hurt very badly by rumors at one time and was determined never to take gossip and accusations lightly. Whenever someone came to her with a knowing look and those few dangerous words, "Did you hear about . . . ?" she went into action.

"Before you tell me about this person," she interrupted, "let me ask you some questions. What did the person say when you approached them with this news you had heard?"

A blank stare usually followed. Then she continued, "Also, did you ask if they would mind you telling others about it so they could pray about it with them—as I'm sure you're doing?"

Another blank stare, usually followed by a slight stuttering. "Well—yes—of course I'm praying . . ."

"I know you mean well," she went on. "But maybe you should be sure it's okay with them for me to know about this before you tell me. They probably trust you with this information, but they may not feel that good about sharing their problems with others."

She then excused herself and went on with her business, leaving the gossiper feeling two inches tall—but ten feet wiser and more cautious.

The only reason gossip ever goes anywhere is that so many of us choose to tolerate it. If we all let it be known that we are no longer in the rumor-business, churches would be a lot more peaceful.

3. Do I think before I speak? If poor, ignorant Nabal, whose story was told in chapter three, had taken a few minutes to reflect on his words to David's messengers before turning them away in anger, he could have prevented a lot of problems. If he had thought about what the king's protection meant to him and his flock, how much he was indebted to the soldiers for their kindness and how much he would be needing those favors in the future, his initial response would have probably been much more gracious.

But he was quick to speak and slow to think. And in the end it cost him much more than some food and other provisions. If you read the story further, you'll find that it cost him his life just ten days later.

Many conflicts in the church can be prevented if we are willing to think before we speak. Instead of running off at the mouth, saying whatever is on our mind in the middle of a dispute, we need to bite our tongue and gather our thoughts. James said, "Everyone should be quick to listen, slow to speak and slow to become angry, for man's anger does not bring about the righteous life that God desires" (1:19-20).

Peacekeepers think before they speak.

Of Wisdom and Character

The next few questions lead us into other issues of character.

4. Do I live a peaceful, genuine life? Isaiah says,

The fruit of righteousness will be peace;

the effect of righteousness will be quietness and confidence forever. (32:17)

Living a peaceful, godly life is the surest way I know of to keep conflict at arm's length. Wouldn't it be wonderful if all of God's people committed themselves to that? How great it would be if every Christian took to heart Paul's admonition to live at peace with everyone whenever possible (Romans 12:18), if every one of us lived quietly and righteously and peacefully.

I can think of several peacemakers in churches I've attended. Charla, an elder's wife, exudes a calm, gentle attitude. I've never heard a negative word come out of her mouth. Her spirit is sweet and gentle. Conflicts seem never to arise in her company.

Janell, who used to teach my daughter's Sunday-school class, is a quiet, peaceful person as well. While others are fighting and arguing, she sits on the floor singing songs about Jesus to our children. And conflict simply has no foothold when she's around.

At the heart of every peacemaker is a calm spirit and pure mind. Peacemakers are able to encourage peace among others because they've found peace deep within themselves.

That's the kind of life I want to lead. That's the kind of person I want to be!

5. Am I alert to trouble? A problem of miscommunication once arose in our former church, and we didn't handle it very well. Two people working in the same ministry, but on different projects, both requested funds for materials. The budget committee made the mistake of assuming that the two requests were overlapping ones—two purchase orders for the same project— so we paid one and threw the other away. It was an honest mistake, but the person who didn't receive her money assumed that her request had been denied. Further, she assumed that the other person in the ministry had something to do with its denial.

Soon afterward we heard of the misunderstanding, but we were slow to deal with it. We thought the person whose request was neglected would simply put in a new request, and after a while we simply forgot the matter. But she didn't. Feeling she had been snubbed, she let the grievance simmer. Before we knew it, people were calling us at home, wondering why we had been so thoughtless and why we were sitting so tight on the church's money. Naturally, most of the people who were upset had most of the facts wrong.

The matter was resolved rather simply. We called the woman in, explained our mistake and provided the funds. But by the time we did, too many rumors and accusations had been flying. Had we been more alert and quicker to respond, a lot of hurt feelings would have been prevented. Our mistake was to expect the woman to make the first move; as we waited the matter blew way out of proportion.

We all do well to stay alert, keeping a keen eye out for potential problems. In times of conflict we need to take initiative to open lines of communication as quickly and kindly as possible.

6. *Am I open-minded?* I like to think of myself as an effective change-agent. I think I have a good sense of what should and shouldn't be changed in our churches to reach the lost of our community. I understand the mindset of today's baby boomers; I am one of them. And I'm convinced that long-range plans for renewal are the key to keeping our churches alive and growing.

But I'm seeing clearly these days that not everyone buys my arguments. It's hard for me to believe that anyone could disagree with my well-researched ideas and conclusions. I'm so convinced that I'm right, that my data is accurate and on target, that I have a hard time dealing with those who simply don't agree with me.

Worse, some of these people have arguments of their own. And as hard as it is to admit, some of their arguments make as much sense as mine do.

I still think I'm right. Maybe I need more data!

The point here is, I've often been anything but open-minded when arguing the case for renewal. Some of my allies have been just as adamant and close-minded as I have. And some in the other camp have been pretty stubborn as well.

If we are to keep peace in the church, it is a must that every one of us remain open to discussion and open to differing viewpoints. That's not easy to do when you're as opinionated as I am.

Peacekeepers don't kowtow to others and shrink back from giving their opinions. But they are always open-minded. And being open-minded means being willing to change our minds and our opinions when we find we are wrong.

7. Do I pray for peace and unity in my church? Ruthie and I were having dinner one evening with some dear friends from the church. It was during the time that the conflict in our church was in full swing. Several people had left, and more were planning to leave. Many of us were anticipating a split in the near future.

As we sat discussing the problems after dinner, our thoughts took a very negative turn. Quite frankly, we were no longer talking, we were griping and gossiping. When conflicts are raging, it's an easy trap to get caught in.

In the middle of the complaining, my friend stopped and said, "I think we need to pray about it." We all knew he meant complaining wasn't doing anyone any good—not us or the church.

Then and there we bowed for a long, earnest prayer. As the four of us joined hands and took turns expressing our concerns to the Lord, a feeling of unity and purpose came over us. Though we didn't speak of it, we all felt it. And our prayers took on a new dimension—a new fervency.

Afterward we were all sorry we'd let ourselves get caught up in petty, meaningless gossip before doing what we should have been doing all along. And we were thankful that my friend had had the heart to remind us.

The greatest thing we can do for the cause of unity in our

church is to pray earnestly, honestly and often.

☐ *We need to pray for guidance.* That God will guide our thoughts and actions and attitudes. That God will guide our church in its work for him.

☐ *We need to pray for wisdom.* On our own we are destined to do the wrong things, think the wrong things, come to the wrong conclusions about what to do for peace. Only God's wisdom can see us through our struggles.

☐ *We need to pray for our leaders.* Our pastors and elders need the prayers of those under their care. They need it as they lead us, and we need it because what they do affects us.

☐ W*e need to pray for our brothers and sisters in Christ.* If we keep members of our church family in our prayers and on our hearts, we will feel a greater kinship with them. We will feel more like a family. And we will be inviting God's wonderful hand of peace on our congregation.

☐ *We need to pray for unity.* Jesus prayed a wonderful prayer for peace—a prayer that is an example and reminder to us as we pray for our church family:

> I have given them the glory that you gave me, that they may be one as we are one: I in them and you in me. May they be brought to complete unity to let the world know that you sent me and have loved them even as you have loved me. (John 17:22-23)

Unity was on the lips and heart of Christ during his days on earth, and it should remain on ours as well. If Jesus prayed for it, let's do all we can to work toward it.

You and I can be God's ambassadors for peace and unity. But only if we pledge our lives, our hearts, our tongues, our minds, our actions, our attitudes and our prayers to the cause.

15

DON'T FORGET THE REAL ENEMY

*D*uring the time of our most heated conflict, our church scheduled many unfruitful meetings. The intent was always to listen to one another and find a compromise among the many differing views and opinions, but it seldom worked out the way we had all hoped. The leaders did an admirable job of trying to keep things under control, but often to no avail. Invariably someone would begin launching verbal attacks on the elders and pastoral team, and someone else would chime in to add to or refute those criticisms. Before long everyone, it seemed, wanted to get in their two-cents worth. The conflict would escalate, and we would disband with very little progress toward compromise.

One such meeting eventually became so brutal and mean-spirited that it sent every one of us home numb, wondering if we would ever bring the conflicts to a decent closure. We now realize that meeting was the catalyst for the split that occurred several weeks later.

Each time a meeting was called, we hoped it would be the one that finally found a middle ground—some compromise that everyone could live with. Sadly, it never happened.

Satan's Playground

After one of the more heated debates, I was having lunch with Rick, a good friend in the faith. Rick told me of the pain he felt while sitting in the meeting the previous day.

"I could almost picture Satan and his demons dancing around the room as we argued," he said. "You know, Satan lives for those days that he can cause dissension among God's people—when he can keep us so busy fighting and arguing and focusing on ourselves that we forget about all the people who need saving."

He stopped to gather his thoughts before continuing. "You know, people are dying and going to hell every day. Within a mile of our building are hundreds, even thousands of lost souls. Most of these people will live and die never having a relationship with the Lord. And right in the middle of it all, we sit arguing over what songs we're going to sing in the assembly and whether the children's classes are good enough! Satan is having the time of his life with us, and we don't even know it."

What a powerful perspective Rick had on our petty quarreling. And he is as right as he can be.

When we fight and argue with each other over petty differences, we are playing right into the hands of Satan. We're doing more to further his cause than non-Christians who attack the church. Satan thrives on keeping us focused inward on our own selfish wants and wishes. And he lives for the day that churches divide and splinter.

I've seen Satan tear apart churches with conflict too many times. I've seen him bring strife and dissension into the most peaceful churches. The thought of it makes me want to repent for every minute I've spent arguing and complaining over petty disagreements with a brother or sister in Christ. May God forgive me for every harsh and harmful word I've ever spoken about a fellow believer. And I pray forgiveness for each moment I've spent complaining about church instead of reaching out to people in need of Christ.

As long as there is even one lost person in the world, one person who has not heard the good news of Jesus, I want to be busy doing whatever I can to bring him or her to Christ. I don't want to let anything deter me from remembering—and carrying out—the Lord's call to "go . . . and make disciples" (Matthew 28:19).

Recognizing the Enemy

Whenever conflict arises in my presence, whenever I feel slighted by a brother or wronged by a fellow deacon or put down by a sister, I pray that I will have the wisdom and strength to overcome my desires to get even.

And I hope to remember the real culprit behind the problems. My quarrel is with Satan and his pesky demons, not my brothers and sisters in Christ. He is the one to blame—the author of all evil and the instigator of all unrest.

There doesn't have to be war in the pews. We don't have to let Satan dictate how we feel and act toward others.

The people of God can look to God for guidance and wisdom. We can look to him for resolution of our conflicts. We can rise above the pettiness and let God take control. Let's not give Satan the foothold he needs to create division. Let's instead look to God.

Whenever we feel tempted to give in to our evil desires and engage in petty conflict, let's instead think of the message from James:

Who is wise and understanding among you? Let him show
it by his good life, by deeds done in the humility that comes
from wisdom. But if you harbor bitter envy and selfish
ambition in your hearts, do not boast about it or deny the
truth. Such "wisdom" does not come down from heaven but
is earthly, unspiritual, of the devil. For where you have envy
and selfish ambition, there you find disorder and every evil
practice.

But the wisdom that comes from heaven is first of all pure;
then peace-loving, considerate, submissive, full of mercy and
good fruit, impartial and sincere. Peacemakers who sow in
peace raise a harvest of righteousness. (3:13-17)

For the cause of Christ to move forward in our churches, each
one of us needs to take ownership of these words. We need to
claim them as our own during times of turmoil—as the peace-
buster busters' national slogan.

A Call to Action

At the end of his book *Twenty Hot Potatoes Christians Are Afraid to
Touch* Tony Campolo makes a plea for action among the Christian community. "Too often," he writes, "when all is said and
done, it has mostly been said. I hope that what I have to say in
this book will do more than just stimulate discussion and controversy. I hope that it will create changes in lifestyles."[1]

Every writer's worst nightmare is that what he or she writes
will fall on deaf ears—or simply be read and then filed away on
a bookshelf somewhere, never to be given a second thought. If
we thought we couldn't make a difference in the world, most of
us would give up writing. On the whole, we're an idealistic lot.

We write because we see things that need to be said. Sometimes we take ourselves too seriously, other times too lightly. But
almost always we feel a passion for the message we're trying to
promote.

The need for churches to stay focused and stop fighting is a message I feel very passionate about. This book is my soapbox, and my voice has now gone raw from months of preaching.

But like Tony Campolo, I don't want to close without giving one last altar call—one final call to action. If the church would only heed Christ's plea for unity and peace, Christians would see revival like none other in the history of the church. We'd be so full of God's power that we wouldn't know what to do with ourselves. Our message of love would stun the world.

Please don't put this book away if you haven't yet asked yourself a few important questions: What have I done to promote unity in my church? Am I part of the problem? Do I cause more problems than I cure? If so, am I willing to do something about it? Am I willing to do whatever I need to do to become an agent of peace and unity?

May we all be among the peacemakers who are known as God's children (Matthew 5:9). May we do our part to put an end to the war in the pews.

Appendix A: For Further Reading

Adams, Jay E. *Sibling Rivalry in the Household of God.* Denver: Accent Books, 1988.

Anderson, Leith. *A Church for the 21st Century.* Minneapolis: Bethany House, 1992.

Anderson, Lynn. *Navigating the Winds of Change.* West Monroe, La.: Howard, 1994.

Anderson, Neil T., and Charles Mylander. *Setting Your Church Free.* Ventura, Calif.: Regal Books, 1994.

Augsburg, David. *When Caring Is Not Enough.* Ventura, Calif.: Regal Books, 1983.

Bacher, Robert, Judith McWilliams and Allan Jahsmann, eds. *Congregational Conflict: A Guide to Reconciliation.* Philadelphia: Parish Life, 1982.

Barna, George. *Finding a Church You Can Call Home.* Ventura, Calif.: Regal Books, 1992.

_____. *The Power of Vision.* Ventura, Calif.: Regal Books, 1992.

Bercovitch, Jacob. *Social Conflicts and Third Parties: Strategies of Conflict Resolution.* Boulder, Colo.: Westview, 1984.

Deutsch, Morton. *The Resolution of Conflict: Constructive and Destructive Processes.* New Haven, Conn.: Yale University Press, 1973.

Flynn, Leslie B. *When the Saints Come Storming In.* Wheaton, Ill.: Victor Books, 1992.

Friedman, Edwin. *Generation to Generation: Family Process in Church and Synagogue.* New York: Guilford, 1985.

Gunnink, Jerrien. *Preaching For Recovery in a Strife-Torn Church.* Grand Rapids, Mich.: Zondervan, 1989.

Halverstadt, Hugh F. *Managing Church Conflict.* Louisville, Ky.: Westminster/John Knox, 1991.

Haugk, Kenneth. *Antagonists in the Church: How to Identify and Deal with Destructive Conflict.* Minneapolis: Augsburg, 1988.

Leas, Speed B. *Leadership and Conflict.* Nashville: Abingdon, 1982.

Leas, Speed B., and Paul Kittlaus. *Church Fights.* Philadelphia: Westminster Press, 1973.

Mickey, Paul, and Robert Wilson. *Conflict and Resolution.* Nashville: Abingdon, 1973.

Sittser, Gerald L. *Loving Across Our Differences.* Downers Grove, Ill.: InterVarsity Press, 1994.

Walton, Richard E. *Managing Conflict: Interpersonal Dialogue and Third Party Roles.* 2nd ed. Reading, Mass.: Addison-Wesley, 1987.

Appendix B: Organizations That Can Help

For information, referrals, seminars and resources:
The Alban Institute
4550 Montgomery Ave., Suite 433 North
Bethesda, MD 20814
(800) 486-1318, extension 229

David Augsburg
Fuller Theological Seminary
135 North Oakland Ave.
Pasadena, CA 91102
(818) 584-5200

Christian Solutions Counseling Services
487 Woodman Rd., Suite 101
Colorado Springs, CO 80919
(719) 528-5682

Counseling and Mediation Center
334 North Topeka
Wichita, KS 67202
(316) 269-2322

Empowered Ministries (church growth and renewal)
P.O. Box 117
Warm Springs, VA 24484
(703) 839-5199

Focus on the Family Pastoral Ministries
8605 Explorer Dr.
Colorado Springs, CO 80920
(719) 531-3360

Freedom in Christ Ministries
491 E. Lambert Rd.
La Habra, CA 90631
(310) 691-9128

Richard Gorsuch
Fuller Theological Seminary
135 North Oakland Ave.
Pasadena, CA 91102
(818) 584-5527; fax (818) 584-9630

Institute for Christian Conciliation
1537 Ave. D, Suite 352
Billings, MT 59102
(406) 256-1583

Lombard Mennonite Peace Center
528 East Madison
Lombard, IL 60148
(708) 627-5310

H. Newton Malony
Fuller Theological Seminary
135 North Oakland Ave.
Pasadena, CA 91102
(818) 584-5528

Mennonite and Brethren in Christ
  Conciliation Services of Canada
50 Kent Ave.
Kitchener, ON N2G 3R1, Canada
(519) 745-8458

Mennonite Conciliation Service
21 South 12th St.
P.O. Box 500
Akron, PA 17501
(719) 859-3889

Resources for Resolving Life's Issues
P.O. Box 9673
Colorado Springs, CO 80932
(719) 380-1065

For consulting and training:
MCC International Conciliation Service
Eastern Mennonite College
Harrisonburg, VA 22801
(703) 432-4452

Notes

Chapter 2: Anatomy of a Church Fight
[1]Leslie Flynn, *When the Saints Come Storming In* (Wheaton, Ill.: Victor Books, 1992), p. 12.
[2]Ibid., p. 76.
[3]Gerald L. Sittser, *Loving Across Our Differences* (Downers Grove, Ill.: InterVarsity Press, 1994), p. 13.
[4]Jerrien Gunnink, *Preaching for Recovery in a Strife-Torn Church* (Grand Rapids, Mich.: Zondervan, 1989), p. 11.
[5]Hugh F. Halverstadt, *Managing Church Conflict* (Louisville, Ky.: Westminster/John Knox, 1991), p. 2.
[6]Speed Leas and Paul Kittlaus, *Church Fights* (Philadelphia: Westminster Press, 1973), p. 72.
[7]Halverstadt, *Managing Church Conflict*, pp. 3-4.
[8]Richard Wolf, *Man at the Top* (Wheaton, Ill.: Tyndale House, 1969), p. 77.

Chapter 3: The One-Minute Conflict Manager
[1]Karen Jordan, "Keys and the Kingdom," *Moody*, April 1994, p. 20.
[2]Charles Colson with Ellen Santilli Vaughn, *The Body* (Dallas: Word, 1992), p. 116.

Chapter 4: Holding Yourself Together When Your Church Is Falling Apart
[1]Simon J. Dahlman, "Why Do People Go?" *Moody*, May 1994, p. 22.

Chapter 5: Step One: Retreat and Regroup
[1]Bill Hybels, *Too Busy Not to Pray* (Downers Grove, Ill.: InterVarsity Press, 1988), pp. 88-89.

Chapter 6: Reassess Your Priorities, Part 1
[1]Rubel Shelley, "Faith Must Be Personal," *Wineskins* 2, no. 3 (1993): 7.
[2]Lee Strobel, *Inside the Mind of Unchurched Harry and Mary* (Grand Rapids, Mich.: Zondervan, 1993), pp. 72-73.

Chapter 7: Reassess Your Priorities, Part 2

[1]George Barna, *The Power of Vision* (Ventura, Calif.: Regal Books, 1992), p. 12.

[2]Lee Strobel, *Inside the Mind of Unchurched Harry and Mary* (Grand Rapids, Mich.: Zondervan, 1993), p. 162.

[3]Barna, *Power of Vision*, p. 69.

[4]Jerrien Gunnink, *Preaching for Recovery in a Strife-Torn Church* (Grand Rapids, Mich.: Zondervan, 1989), p. 23.

[5]Leith Anderson, *A Church for the 21st Century* (Minneapolis: Bethany House, 1992), pp. 63-64.

[6]Barna, *Power of Vision*, p. 47.

Chapter 8: Reassess Your Priorities, Part 3

[1]Tony Campolo, *How to Be Pentecostal Without Speaking in Tongues* (Dallas: Word, 1991), pp. 34-35.

Chapter 9: Step Three: Go to Your Knees

[1]Charles F. Stanley, *Handle with Prayer* (Wheaton, Ill.: Victor Books, 1982), p. 8.

[2]Ibid., pp. 7-8.

[3]Bill Hybels, *Too Busy Not to Pray* (Downers Grove, Ill.: InterVarsity Press, 1988), pp. 118-19, 121.

[4]Ibid., pp. 125-26.

[5]Lloyd John Ogilvie, *You Can Pray with Power* (Ventura, Calif.: Regal Books, 1988), p. 12.

Chapter 10: Step Four: If You've Decided to Stay . . .

[1]Leonard Sweet, "The Four Fundamentalisms of Old Line Protestants,"*The Christian Century*, March 13, 1985, p. 266.

[2]Wynne Gillis, "Santa's Law . . . and God's Love," *Christian Standard*, December 19, 1982, p. 10.

Chapter 11: Step Five: If You've Decided to Go . . .

[1]Chuck Swindoll, *The Grace Awakening* (Dallas: Word, 1990), pp. 190-91.

[2]George Barna, *Finding a Church You Can Call Home* (Ventura, Calif.: Regal Books, 1992), pp. 40-41.

[3]Tony Campolo, *How to Be Pentecostal Without Speaking in Tongues* (Dallas: Word, 1991), p. 163.

[4]Lee Strobel, *Inside the Mind of Unchurched Harry and Mary* (Grand Rapids, Mich.: Zondervan, 1993), pp. 124-25.

Chapter 12: Step Six: Settle In and Settle Down!

[1]George Barna, *Finding a Church You Can Call Home* (Ventura, Calif.: Regal Books, 1992), p. 140.

[2]Bill Hybels, *Too Busy Not to Pray* (Downers Grove, Ill.: InterVarsity Press, 1988), p. 13.

[3]Karl Menninger with Martin Mayman and Paul Pruyser, *The Vital Balance* (New York: Viking, 1963), p. 22.

[4]Barna, *Finding a Church You Can Call Home*, p. 93.

[5]Douglas L. Fagerstrom and James W. Carlson, *The Lonely Pew* (Grand Rapids, Mich.: Baker Book House, 1993), p. 9.

[6]Charles F. Stanley, *Handle with Prayer* (Wheaton, Ill.: Victor Books, 1982), pp. 58-60.

Chapter 13: Exposing the "Peace-Busters"

[1]Mike Yaconelli, editorial, *The Door* 82 (December 1984/January 1985).

[2]Daniel Taylor, *The Myth of Certainty* (Waco, Tex.: Word, 1986), p. 34.

[3]Chuck Swindoll, *The Grace Awakening* (Dallas: Word, 1990), pp. 81-82.

[4]Paul Harvey, *For What It's Worth* (New York: Bantam Books, 1991), p. 9.

[5]Leith Anderson, *A Church for the 21st Century* (Minneapolis: Bethany House, 1992), p. 145.

[6]Lee Strobel, *Inside the Mind of Unchurched Harry and Mary* (Grand Rapids, Mich.: Zondervan, 1993), pp. 159-60.

[7]Ibid., p. 69.

[8]Leslie Flynn, *When the Saints Come Storming In* (Wheaton, Ill.: Victor Books, 1992), pp. 106-7.

Chapter 15: Don't Forget the Real Enemy

[1]Tony Campolo, *Twenty Hot Potatoes Christians Are Afraid to Touch* (Dallas: Word, 1988), p. 235.